Old print of the well and chapel and the adjacent parish church at Holywell

THE OLD PARISH CHURCHES
OF NORTH WALES

Mike Salter

FOLLY PUBLICATIONS

ACKNOWLEDGEMENTS

The illustrations in this book are mostly the product of the author's own surveys since the 1970s. The plans are all reproduced to a common scale of 1:400, this scale being also used for almost all other churches in the books in this series. A few modern digital pictures are included in this book but the majority of the photographs were taken in black and white by the author during the 1980s. The book also includes old prints and postcards from the author's collections. Kate Miles provided pictures of Dolgellau, Llanegryn, Llanfrothen, Mallwyd, Penmynydd and the Eglwys y Bedd at Caer Gybi. Thanks to Max Barfield, who helped in various ways towards preparing the original 1993 edition of this book, and also to Paul and Allan at Aspect Design for help with the cover design and other artwork matters.

AUTHOR'S NOTES

This book presents information about the architecture, furnishings and monuments up to the year 1800 to be seen in the parish churches of North Wales. Furnishings and monuments dating from after 1800 are not usually included although restorations and the additions of porches and vestries, etc, are usually briefly mentioned in passing.

Visitors are advised to use Ordnance Survey Landranger series 1:50,000 scale maps to find the churches, many of which lie isolated from any village and can be quite hard to locate. Grid references are given in the gazetteers.

The boundaries used are those in force in the early 1990s. Note that in the changes made in the 1970s Denbighshire lost a few parishes east of the River Conwy to Gwynedd but gained a few from the projecting NE corner of Merioneth. The result was rather neater and straighter boundaries than had previously been the case. Currently the eastern parts of Caernarvonshire and the western parts of Denbighshire are included in the unity authority of Conwy. Using that as a division for this book makes little sense, and the resulting maps would not have fitted so easily onto the pages.

Of necessity some of the place names are shortened or abbreviated on the maps.

This book is dedicated to all those that over the years were members or leaders of The Questors, the youth club of Beckminster Methodist Church, especially those who visited the outdoor pursuits centre at The Towers, near Capel Curig, in the 1970s.

ABOUT THE AUTHOR

Mike Salter is 58 and has been a professional writer and publisher since he went on the Government Enterprise Allowance Scheme for unemployed people in 1988. He is particularly interested in the planning and layout of medieval buildings and has a huge collection of plans of churches and castles he has measured during tours (mostly by bicycle, motorcycle or on foot) throughout all parts of the British Isles since 1968. Wolverhampton born and bred, Mike now lives in an old cottage beside the Malvern Hills. His other interests include walking, maps, railways, board games, all kinds of morris dancing, mumming, playing percussion instruments and calling folk dances.

Copyright 1993 & 2012 by Mike Salter.   This edition published February 2012
The original 72-page first edition of this book was published in April 1993.
Folly Publications, Folly Cottage, 151 West Malvern Rd, Malvern, Worcs, WR14 4AY
Printed by Aspect Design, 89 Newtown Rd, Malvern, Worces WR14 2PD

Talyllyn Church, Merioneth

CONTENTS

INTRODUCTION

Christianity was well established in Wales by the 6th century. The number of churches with raised circular enclosures and the frequent occurrence in place names starting with the suffix Llan, meaning a religious site, shows that numerous chapels existed by the time of the Norman invasion of the late 11th century. Another indication of an early foundation date is a dedication to an obscure saint who was one of the pioneer holy men of the district. Nearly forty churches in Denbighshire, a similar number in Caernarfon and Merioneth combined, and a slightly greater number in Anglesey, but just four in the much more Anglicised district of Flintshire, have evidence of having been founded by the 9th century. By that time the clas system of monastic mother chuches with subsidiary chapels-of-ease had been set up.

Interior of Capel Trillo

Most of these early buildings would have been tiny structures of wood or unmortared stone and no structural remains survive of any of them. Those few churches which had mortared stone walls have been rebuilt and extended out of existence during the medieval and later centuries. The tiny chapel of St Trillo at Llandrillo-yn-Rhos is probably 13th century in its present form but it does give a good idea of the nature of many of the minor chapels, a dark single chamber just big enough to contain an altar and an attendant priest. Other relics of this early period are broken remnants of grave slabs and crosses, the early 9th century Pillar of Eliseg, although now only half its original length, being the best of the crosses.

Interior of Tywyn Church

Llansilin Church

Relics of the 12th century are generally not very common or of much significance in churches on the mainland of North Wales. Quite a number of fonts remain, most of them plain, but some have simple ornamentation such as a cable band, a row of beads, or a few chevrons. Apart from the odd dubious arch or short length of plain walling nothing remains standing of 12th century churches in Clwyd, and not much in mainland Gwynnedd, but about a dozen churches on Anglesey retain a 12th century nave, usually with one small round-headed window or a plain doorway, perhaps blocked, still remaining. The nave of c1140 at Penmon gives an idea of the modest size and dark interiors of these buildings. It was originally provided with a tiny square chancel to contain the altar but in the 1160s that part was replaced by a square central tower with transepts and a larger new chancel further east. Some of the other chapels such as Capel Lligwy has separate chancels too, but others were just a single chamber. Even now not many medieval North Wales churches have a chancel arch and a structurally separate chancel. The other surviving naves on Anglesey may be later than that at Penmon, say 1160 to 1200, and there is little evidence of much building or rebuilding in North Wales parochial churches earlier than that.

The only parochial church retaining evidence of aisles earlier than c1200 is Tywyn, where the aisles were originally of four bays with round arches on circular columns. In the 13th century this church was made cruciform with the addition of a central tower, transepts and a chancel. These survive, but in a much rebuilt state. Corwen retains a transept and chancel of what was probably once a cruciform 13th century church, and Llansilin has fragments of another. Llanaber has a fairly complete and little altered church of c1200-50 consisting of a chancel and a nave with arcades of five pointed arches opening into narrow aisles with a particularly fine south doorway. Llangadwaladr on Anglesey has a roll-moulded doorway. Otherwise, although nearly twenty churches in Clwyd and about thirty churches in Gwynedd have structural remains of the 13th century, the work is plain and modest in size, as in the small nave and chancel church at Llanfair-is-Gaer, and usually has been much altered in later periods. LLanfrothen is an instance of a fairly complete single chamber 13th century church with a single west lancet and three at the east end. It has doorways with voussoirs instead of dressed stones forming an arch which are indicative of an early date, although in Wales such doorways remained in use throughout the 14th century as well.

Interior of Llanaber Church

Arches were usually pointed in the 13th century but the district tended to be conservative and retained the round arch later than in England, where it is little seen after c1200. The round-arched doorway of three chamfered-edged orders of c1180 - 1200 at Aberdaron illustrates the transition between the Romanesque and Gothic styles. At Llanaber the chancel arch capitals are still Romanesque in style, although the arch is pointed. Lancet windows are characteristic of this period, which many restored examples at Llanaber. There are groups of three with the middle light rising higher in gable end walls at Conwy, Corwen and Llanfrothen. A renewed set as late as the 1290s remain at Rhuddlan. Eventually lancets were put together in pairs and the space between the light leads pierced with a circle or a trefoil, as in the chancels at Conwy and Llanaber.

There are, or were, churches of c1290 - 1350 of some size at the places in North Wales which came under English control after the defeat of the Welsh princes in the 1280s. These were the fortified towns of Beaumaris, Caernarfon, Conwy, Flint, Phuddlan and Denbigh and the undefended towns and villages of Gresford, Hawarden, Holt, Ruthin and Wrexham. The churches at Denbigh, Rhuddlan and Ruthin were double naved, ie a nave with a single aisle of similar width, but the other churches followed the more normal English layout with a pair of aisles of more modest width. The church at Flint was entirely rebuilt in 1846 but Speed's map of 1610 suggests it had a similar layout. Most of these churches also had towers, and were thus distinctively different from the humble churches of the surrounding districts where Welsh influence predominated. In Gwynedd very few of the medieval churches have aisles, especially on Anglesey. In Denbigh and Flint before the building boom there of the late 15th and early 16th centuries the only church additional to those list above to have aisles was that of Bangor-is-Coed, once an important monastic centre in Maelor Saesneg. The neighbouring church of Overton has a 14th century tower. On Anglesey there is much minor 14th century work including several instances of where a small single-bodied church was rebuilt without being enlarged either at all or significantly. Newborough is an instance of a planted village of this period with only a modest new church. Windows in this period rarely have the sort of complex floral pattern tracery found in contemporary English churches which have given rise to the style name of Decorated, and none call for especial comment here. There are good 14th century reset windows at Llanbeblig.

Aberdaron, c1180-1200

Holt c1500

Gwalchmai, 16th Century

*CHURCH
DOORWAYS
IN
NORTH WALES*

Llanfechell, c1200

Llangadwaladr, c1661

Work of the early 15th century is again sporadic and mostly minor. On Anglesey there are churches mostly of c1400 at LLandyfrydog, Llanddyfnan and Penmynydd. The insertion of a central tower into the east end of the nave at Hawarden and the rebuilding at Llansilin may perhaps be associated with damage caused during Owain Glyndwr's rebellion. Then from the 1470s onwards until the mid 16th century there was a building boom. Nearly all of the churches have or had windows of that period and there are many fine open roofs with braced trusses, collar-beams and wind-braces sometimes making patterns of quatrefoils and trefoils. Panelled ceilings occur too, especially as a short section or celure to distinguish the altar end of a single chamber from the rest of it. A few older roofs also remain. On Anglesey churches were often re-built in this period without being enlarged, and there are many single chambers entirely or most of this period on the mainland, as at Bryneglwys, Derwen and Llanderfel.

Many churches in the Vale of Clwyd and several in Caernarvonshire were rebuilt in the late medieval period on the so-called double-naved layout in which a second body equal in width, height and usually also length would be added to an original chamber composed of a 12th or 13th century nave later extended at the east end to create a more spacious sanctuary. There are nearly twenty churches of this type in Denbigh-shire and Flintshire, possibly inspired by the wide aisle added to the collegiate church at Ruthin in the 1360s. Abergele has the longest church of this type. Others of note are at Cilcain, Llanefydd, Llanfair Dyffryn Clwyd, Llanynys, St Asaph and Whitchurch (Llanfarchell). Two out of the three churches of this type on Anglesey have been partly dismantled, but there are several on the Llyn peninsular. Most of the double-naved churches in Denbighshire and Flintshire have late medieval towers but they are rarer in Gwynned. Arches during this period are usually the flatter four-centred type. East win-dows are often large and fitted with complex tracery in which verticals predominate, hence the name Perpendicular used to describe the style of this period. The lesser windows in the side walls often have square heads with the lights simply cusped.

The triple-gabled east end of Llangwnnadl Church

Llangwyfan Church, on a tidal island off the Anglesey coast

Gwynnedd has a number of diverse and widely scattered late medieval churches which call for attention. That at Dolwyddellan illustrates that in a sparely populated upland parish a small single chamber would still suffice. Llandegai, of medium size and much rebuilt, is cruciform. Several other churches became cruciform or T-shaped because of the addition of transeptal chapels. Caer Gybi (Holyhead) has transepts and an all-embattled aisled nave with a clerestory, but a tower was only provided later, and then at the west end. Clynnog Fawr has a large embattled nave and chancel with a west tower and transepts. A later passageway joins the church to a spacious detached chantry chapel. On a smaller scale this layout with and without the transepts respectively is repeated in the Anglesey churches of Llandegfan and Llaneilian. Llanbeblig has transepts forming one space with the central crossing as at Clynnog Fawr. Llangwnnadl was widened into a triple-naved church, a plain rectangle wider than it is long and without a separate chancel, porch or tower.

Llanfaelrhys: 12th century font   *Llangwnnadl: font, c1520*   *Llanrwst: font, 17th century*

The east end of Llanrhaeadr-yng-Nghinmeirch Church

Tower at Bodfari

The east end of Llanefydd Church

Corbel at Caerhun

In Denbighshire and Flintshire there are a several churches which were rebuilt under the patronage of Sir William Stanley, a powerful lord who held the lordship of Bromfield from 1483 until his execution in 1495, and his third wife Margaret Beaufort, Countess of Richmond and Derby, and mother of the then reigning monarch, Henry VII. Wiliam and Margaret had a hand in the rebuilding works at Gresford, Holt, Hope, Mold and Wrexham and the re-roofing at Ruthin. At Holywell they built a chapel of St Winefride above a remarkable star-shaped holy well just west of the parish church. Ffynon Fair has a similar star-shaped holy well within a ruined chapel. Taking architecture, furnishings and monuments together Gresford scarcely has an equal amongst medieval non-monastic parish churches in Wales. Wrexham has the largest parochial church in North Wales and is also quite splendid. It has an east apse like the well-chapel at Holywell. The towers at Gresford and Wrexham are particularly impressive, with blank panelling, niches for statues, and pinnacles. The Wrexham tower may have been completed in the 1520s but at Gresford the work dragged on until the 1560s, ie after the Reformation. Other towers still of medieval appearance are known to be quite late in date. That at Northop seems to have only been completed in the 1570s and that at Llandrillo-yn-Rhos was only begun c1552. Finally the aisled nave and west tower at Hanmer should be mentioned as an instance of good (but not exceptional) late medieval work similar to that found in churches in the adjacent parts of Shropshire and Cheshire.

By the 1540s the original bare and dimly-lighted 12th and 13th century church interiors had been transformed. Large new windows pierced through the old walls and provided in the later extensions admitted more light despite some of them being filled with stained glass depicting bibical scenes, lives of saints and heraldry of benefacrtors. Gresford has a particularly fine set of stained glass windows of c1495 - 1540, and there are stained glass Jesse Trees of the same date at Disserth and Llanrhaeadr-yng-Nghinmeirch. There are fragments of an earlier Jesse Tree at Worthenbury and several other churches retain the odd stained glass figure of a saint or a shield of a patron in a tracery light. Flagstones and tiles were introduced in the late medieval period, but some churches retained until the 19th century their original floors of rammed earth, which were recovered once a year at harvest time with fresh rushes. Gradually benches were provided for the congregation, and a pulpit for the preaching of sermons. Wrexham has a brass lectern of c1520. There are choir stalls with hinged seats or misericords at Beaumaris and Gresford, the latter set backing onto parclose screens.

A chancel was usually divided off from the nave by a screen above which there was sometimes a loft used by musicians and actors. Organs were unknown in village churches in the medieval period and plays were of importance in conveying God's Word to congregations before sermons became fashionable and services were held in English or Welsh rather than in Latin. The screens at Derwen, LLanegryn, Llaneilian, Llanengan, and Llanrwst retain their lofts. There are other screens of note without lofts at Abergele, Clogaenog, Conwy and Gresford. Much woodwork was painted and combined with murals and painted ceilings to produce a riot of rich colours. Damaged wall paintings have survived or been discovered hidden under numerous coats of whitewash during restoration at a few churches, as at Llangar and Llanynys. Plate used during services was usually kept in a locked chest and these were often made by hollowing out a complete trunk. The piscinae found in chancels and other parts of churches where altars were set up were used for draining and rinsing out chalices used during masses. The more important churches usually had stone seats for priests set into the south wall of the chancel, as at Clynnog Fawr. Late medieval fonts are quite common and are normally octagonal with a quatrefoil, fleur-de-lys, heraldic shield or beast either incised or in shallow relief on each face. Earlier fonts are usually circular bowls, plain or with a few basic decorative motifs in relief.

Sedilia at Clynnog Fawr

Chancel screen and rood-loft at Llanrwst

On the whole work of the late 16th and 17th centuries is more common in North Wales than in England, although the only new foundations were the small manorial chapels of Gwydir and Rug and the Earl of Leicester's huge new incomplete church of 1578 at Denbigh. Side chapels are common additions in Gwynedd. They contained secondary or chantry altars until the Reformation of the 1540s and provided space for private seating for the patron's family. Some churches, as at Llandudwen and Nant Peris, ended up with a family chapel on either side of the east end, producing a T-shaped plan. Most of these chapels are modest single bay structures almost square in plan but Llanrwst and Llangadwaladr have chapels on a more ambitious scale of the 1630s and 1660s respectively. Porches are commonly of the period 1540 to 1700 and there are a few towers, mostly plain and humble like those of Caer Gybi and Llanfor. During this period churches were stripped of images and other features which were

Rug Chapel

offensive to the reformed Church. Carved fragments from screens and lofts removed then or later sometimes found their way into new fittings such as pulpits, of which there are quite a few dating from this era, or stalls, benches, chests, altar tables and reredoses. Medieval stone altar slabs were usually replaced by communion tables. Window tracery and cusping of the lights (as at Llanrwst) rarely occurs during this period, when square-headed or round-headed lights under a flat hoodmould are the norm.

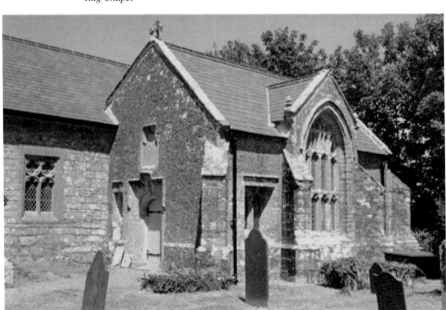

The south chapel at Llangadwaladr

Although the tower at Mold as rebuilt in 1768-73 is in a sort of slightly debased Gothic style, the Classical style using the round arch was in favour for much of the 18th century. The church of 1742 at Berse Drelincourt has been much altered, but there are west towers at Llangollen and Bangor-is-Coed. The latter was part of a remodelling of the 1720s by Richard Trubshaw, who in 1736-9 oversaw the construction at Worthenbury of what is now the best preserved church of this period in Wales. It is of brick with stone used for the corners, windows and doorways, and details such as the balustrading and urns on the tower. The church of 1769 at Holywell has two storey elevations to accommodate galleries. Both here and at Merchweil, of 1778, east apses were added on later. Generally though, 18th century work in churches is restricted to minor repairs, the addition of a vestry or chapel, or the insertion of a new window or two.

Tower at Gresford Church

Rebuildings and restorations of the churches began in earnest in the early 19th century and continued until the First World War. A few churches managed to escape lightly. Others were entirely rebuilt except perhaps for a tower or side chapel judged to have survived two centuries of neglect better than the rest of the fabric. Sometimes a window or doorway was considered worth saving and was reset into newer walling. Many churches were thoroughly repaired, their walls scraped, and many of the furnishings replaced, so that their character has changed even though much of the walling and most of the roofs may still be medieval. However there are many North Wales churches still possessing much woodwork of the period 1400 to 1800 when roof trusses, ceilings, screens, pulpits, altar rails, panelling, stalls, benches and pews are all taken into account. Indeed many churches in Gwynedd are more notable for their wooden fittings and furnishings rather than for ancient architectural features of stone.

Bangor Is-coed Church

Effigies at Llanarmon yn-Ial

The parish churches of Gwynedd are rather lacking in monumental effigies. There are 14th century knights at Betws-y-Coed, Dolgellau, Llanuwchllyn and Tywyn. plus a lady of c1240 at Beaumaris. The Betws-y-Coed and LLanuwchllyn effigies probably came from a short-lived Flintshire workshop that also produced c1400 the light relief figures of saints donated by Gruffudd ap Gwilym to the Anglesey churches of Llani-estyn and Llanbabo. This workshop may also have produced the effigy of a priest at Newborough. The majority of medieval effigies in North Wales, and especially those of the 13th and 14th centuries, lay in the churches of monastic houses and the cathe-drals of Bangor and St Asaph. The Beaumaris effigies and later knights and their wives at Llandegai and Penmynydd are in fact refugees from the former Franciscan friary church of Llanfaes, near Beaumaris. These later effigies and the tombs they lay upon were made of alabaster in the east midlands of England.

The Clywd valley had a school of sculptors from the mid 13th century until the end of the 14th and parish churches there contain over twenty effigies of that period, some of them now fragmentary. Three of them lie at Gresford, which has a fine collection of monuments, another four are at Northop, and Llanarmon-yn-Ial, Ruthin and Tremeir-chion each have two, the priest at the latter being under a fine canopied recess. Other recesses for effigies which have gone can be seen at Conwy and several other places. Rhuddlan has an incised slab of a late 13th century bishop. Ruabon has a fine tomb of the 1520s with effigies of a knight and his wife, whilst Whitchurch has monuments of the 1560s and 1580s, the former heralding the new Classical ideas of the Renaissance. A 15th century priest at Corwen and knights of the 1590s and 1640s at Gresford and Llanarmon-yn-Ial have the middle part of the body left solid, only the bust and legs being shown. Most of the 17th century effigies are small kneeling mural figures set on either side of a prayer desk with smaller figures of children behind the adults.

Monument at Nannerch

Monument at Gresford

Tomb chest at Ruabon

Brass at Llanrwst

Monumental brasses are more numerous in North Wales than in other parts of the principality. The oldest is a small plate of c1500 at Llanbeblig mostly filled with an inscription but having a tiny scene of a man in bed, more a curiosity than a great work of art. There are cut-out later standing figures at Clynnog Fawr and Ruthin, and kneeling figures at Beaumaris and Dolwyddelan. Single plates have depictions of family groups at Llanwenllwyfo, Ruthin and Whitchurch, and a plate at Mold depicts just a single tiny figure. Brasses of the 1660s at Holt and Wrexham have various motifs with the inscriptions but no figures. This reflects a general trend as the 17th century wore on towards mural tablets sometimes just with plain inscriptions, and without any sort of effigy, but often having symbols of death, or a person's trade, status, rank or claim to fame. Just occasionaly there are more ambitious monuments adorned with cherubs, coats-of-arms, and architectural surrounds with columns and pediments, etc.

GAZETTEER OF CHURCHES ON THE ISLE OF ANGLESEY

ABERFFRAW   *St Bueno*   SH 353688

The south and west walls of the nave are of the 12th century when the rulers of Gwynedd had a royal palace here. Reset on the inside of west wall of the nave is an arch made up from material probably from the western face of a chancel arch of that period adorned with chevrons and the heads of rams and bulls. In later years this reset arch may have opened into a west tower, mentioned as long gone in 1833. A new chancel as wide as the nave and a north aisle of similar width were added in the 16th century, and the roofs date from then. Except for the 14th century south doorway the openings are 19th century when the outer walls were mostly rebuilt above the foundations and a small vestry added at the NW corner. The four bay arcade has two octagonal piers and a wider central one. The octagonal font is 13th century.

AMLWCH   *St Eleth*   SH 442929

A church of 1800 by James Wyatt has replaced the cruciform medieval church with a west tower. The oldest monuments are those to Captain David Lloyd, d1641, and Howell Lewis, d1683.

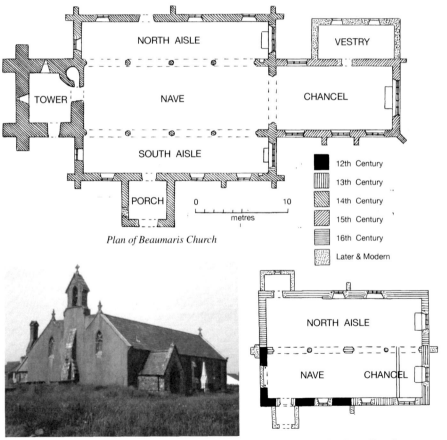

Plan of Beaumaris Church

12th Century
13th Century
14th Century
15th Century
16th Century
Later & Modern

Aberffraw Church

Plan of Aberffraw Church

Beaumaris Church

BEAUMARIS   *St Mary and St Nicholas*   SH 601762

Beaumaris was founded in the 1290s as an English garrison town and has an early 14th century church more akin to those of central England than is usual in this part of Wales. It has an angle-buttressed west tower with low corner pinnacles. The church has a spacious interior with four bay arcades to the aisles and a low chancel arch with foliage stops. The doorways, south porch, several windows and the piscinae in the aisles are original. In c1500 the south aisle walls were raised and embattled and both aisles given new east windows whilst the chancel was rebuilt at least one bay longer than before and given a five-light east window and tall pinnacles. On the north side there are two windows of c1600 above the vestry, which is a Victorian replacement of the original. The nave clerestory also has windows of c1600 on the north side, but original quatrefoil-shaped windows remain on the south side. The tower battlements are of c1500 but sit on a rebuilt belfry stage of 1825 containing the only full set of bells on Anglesey. The north aisle was only heightened in the 1820s to take a set of galleries, now removed. Some of the old bosses are re-used in the new roof.

There are misericords on the choir stalls which may have come from nearby Llanfaes Friary in the 1530s. Also from the friary is the coffin lid bearing a floriated stem carrying a half effigy of Princess Joanna, daughter of King John and wife of Llywelyn ap Gruffydd, d1237. There is an alabaster tomb with effigies of William Bulkeley, c1490, and his wife Elin. A brass has kneeling effigies of Richard and Elizabeth Bulkeley, d1530. Other memorials are to Sir Henry Sidney, d1583, Anne Owen, d1604, Margaret Jones of Castellmarch, d1609, Dr Thomas Caesar, d1632, Margaret Hughes, d1697, Captain Hugh Williams, d1795, plus several others of later date.

Bodedern Church

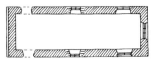

Plan of Bodwrog Church

BODEDERN   *St Edeyrn*   SH 334804

The long nave has a 14th century north door-way with wave mouldings. Both it and the chancel added in the 15th century were mostly rebuilt in 1871. Original late medieval features are the south doorway in a moulded frame, the east window, the windows with pairs of cin-quefoiled lights in the nave, the octagonal font, and the roofs. The north transept of 1871 con-tains a 6th century inscribed stone.

Chancel arch, Eglwys y Bedd at Caer Gybi

BODEWRYD   *St Mary*   SH 400907

The small 15th century single chamber with a late 16th century three-light east window is entered through a doorway of c1500 reset in a north transeptal porch.

BODWROG   *St Twrog*   SH 401776

The good south and north doorways (the latter now a window) and the east window with panel tracery and the SE window of the single chamber are all late 15th century. The font must be older, and perhaps some of the walling. The bull's head of the Bulke-ley family of Beaumaris appears over the south doorway, which has carved spandrels between the four-centred head and an outer frame. The pulpit and reading desk are late 18th or early 19th century.

Caer Gybi Church

CAER GYBI (HOLYHEAD) *St Cybi* SH 247827

The churchyard is enclosed by the ruined walls of a Roman fort which must have been handed over to the church at quite an early date. Here the ancient clas or monastery then founded survived through to the Reformation in the form of a college. The transepts and a crossing probably intended to carry a central tower are of c1480. The nave and aisles with a low embattled clerestory above the three bay arcades and the fan-vaulted south porch and the polygonal staircase turret to the former rood loft adjoining the south transept are of c1500-20. However, 13th century walling with one original lancet survives in the chancel. The south doorway has statue niches on either side and the royal shield appears in the left spandrel, whilst there are saints in the jambs and a God the Father above. The nave roof has been rebuilt with the old materials. There are angels above the arcade piers. The south chapel now dates entirely from the restoration of 1877-9 and most of the other chancel features are of that date except the 14th century east window. The plain and oblong west tower of the 17th century is partly built above the fort wall, and a Victorian vestry adjoins the north side of it.

On the south side of the churchyard is the Eglwys Y Bedd or Chapel of the Dead. The windows are of the 18th century, when it was made into a school. The arch remains of a lost chancel.

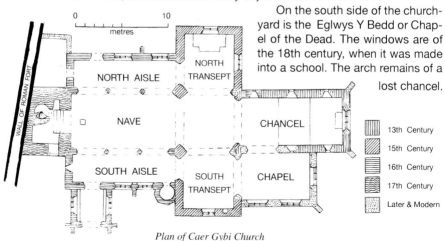

13th Century
15th Century
16th Century
17th Century
Later & Modern

Plan of Caer Gybi Church

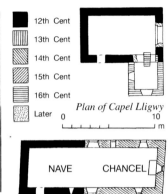

■	12th Cent
▥	13th Cent
▨	14th Cent
▧	15th Cent
▤	16th Cent
▦	Later

Plan of Capel Lligwy
0   10
└─┴─┴─┴─┴─┘ m

NAVE   CHANCEL

Capel Lligwy

Plan of Llanbabo Church

CAPEL LLIGWY   SH 499863

This small ruined chapel in the care of Cadw has a round-arched 12th century south doorway. The bellcote is later and the tiny south chapel with west and south windows and the east window of the main chamber are 16th century.

CERRIG CEINWEN   *St Ceinwen*   SH 424737

The church lies by a holy well and was rebuilt in 1860 but it has a 12th century font with panels of interlacing, crosses and knots. The inner lintel of the south doorway is a reused 12th century slab incised with a petalled cross in a circle and there is also the upper part of an 11th century (or earlier) cross-shaft incised with a similar motif.

COEDANA   *St Aneu*   SH 431821

The church was rebuilt in 1894 but has a circular font bearing the date 1702.

GWALCHMAI   *St Morhaiarn*   SH 391761

The east window with flowing tracery is a reset 14th century piece from Heneglwys. Added to the north side of the eastern part is a north chapel of c1500 with an arcade of a pair of four-centred arches. The roofs and the south doorway are also of that period. The date 1674 on the east gable records some rebuilding around then. The octagonal font may be 15th century. There is a monument to Richard Lewis, d1725.

Gwalchmai Church

HENEGLWYS   *St Llwydian*   SH 423761

The single chamber was mostly rebuilt in 1845 but there are three 15th century windows, one of which has an older inscribed stone for its sill, and there are two 14th century doorways with reset 12th century voussoirs with lion heads above them. Also 12th century are the stoup and the font with an arcade of columns and depressed arches in relief with flattened Greek key ornamentation above and a crudely carved band of lozenges below. The original east window is now at Gwalchmai.

LLANALGO   *St Gallgo*   SH 501851

The transepts and short chancel are late 15th century. The nave has an old roof but the walling west of the transepts was rebuilt in 1892. There is a late 13th century bell.

LLANBABO   *St Pabo*   SH 378868

A late 14th century relief depicts the 6th century North British king Pabo in a robe set under a canopy. The church was extended to contain his shrine. It was originally 12th century, there being stones with chevrons of that period reset over the south doorway, where there are also three heads of possibly even older origin. The roof with three pairs of jointed crucks and the tapered circular font may also be 12th century.

LLANBADRIG   *St Patrick*   SH 376947

The 12th century font has arcading round the bowl. Still older are two inscribed stones, one with a fish symbol and the other with a wheel-cross and a Latin cross. The nave is 14th century and the longer chancel of the same width appears to be of the 1840s but with the 15th century east window and the adjacent niche reused.

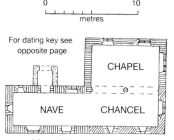

Plan of Gwalchmai Church

LLANBEDR GOCH   *St Peter*   SH 511805

The small main chamber has two 15th century doorways, the northern one flanked by heads of a man and a bishop. The transepts with plain mullioned windows are 17th century. Two panelled bench ends from Llaneilian, one with a mermaid, now form the reading desk and seat. There are memorials to Dr William Lloyd, d1661, Rector of Llaneilian, Anne Morgan, d1675, wife of the bishop of Bangor, and Roger and Catherine Roberts, d1704.

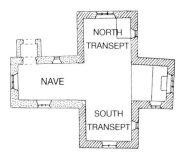

Plan of Llanalgo Church

Llanbedr Goch Church

LLANBEULAN *St Peulan* SH 373755

Although its features are Victorian the nave is probably 12th century as a window-head of that period is reset in the east wall of a 14th century south transept bearing the date 1657, referring to some rebuilding. The chancel and chancel arch are 14th century but the east and south windows are 15th and 16th century respectively. The fine 12th century rectangular font is carved with a ring-cross, bands of chevrons and a rope pattern, chequerwork and a Greek fretwork pattern and blank arcading. The church has been made redundant and is cared for by the Friends of Friendless Churches.

LLANDDANIEL FEB *St Deiniol* SH 495704

The only old features to survive a rebuilding in 1873 are the vestry doorway with a face for a keystone and an heraldic graveslab in the porch.

LLANDDEUSANT *St Marcellus & Marcellinus* SH 346853

Only a 12th century font with blank arcading survived the rebuilding of 1868.

LLANDDONA *St Dona* SH 574809

The nave, chancel and transepts are all of 1873. Older features are the octagonal font, the south doorway of c1500 with creatures carved in the spandrels between the arch and the outer frame, and a datestone of 1566 upside down above the east window.

LLANDDWYN *St Dwynwen* SH 387627

Ruins of a cruciform 16th century church lie on an island in Newborough parish. Fragments of the chancel stand up high. The rest is reduced to foundations.

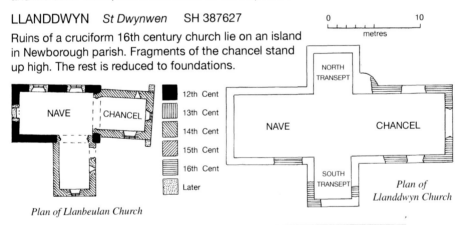

0   10
metres

12th Cent
13th Cent
14th Cent
15th Cent
16th Cent
Later

Plan of Llanbeulan Church

Plan of Llanddwyn Church

Llanddwyn Church

LLANDDYFNAN *St Dyfnan* SH 503787

The 14th century nave has an unusual contemporary western chamber and a north doorway with naked figures (one attacked by a beast) as the stops of the hoodmould. In the 15th century the chancel was rebuilt wider to make it almost square. It has a three-light east window with panel tracery and a south-light south window. Of the same period is the south doorway inserted into the western chamber and now covered by a 19th century porch. The doorway is of yellow freestone and has a round arch with a carved keystone set within a square frame outside of which are niches with St Mary and St John, and the Trinity on top with Christ crucified. The furnishings are of 1846.

LLANDEGFAN *St Tegfan* SH 564744

The main chamber has a 15th century roof with cruck-like trusses but the walling is probably older. The transepts have similar but obviously later roofs so are probably 16th century. The northern one extends to a wide almost square building set at a slight angle which may be a late medieval chantry chapel in origin, although it was later used as a school-room and may have been mostly rebuilt for that purpose. The south porch may be 14th century but has been rebuilt. The west tower is of 1811, the transept windows are of 1847, and the other windows are of 1901-3. The oldest monuments are those to Thomas Davis, d1649, a royal messenger, and William Owen, d1712, erected by his friend Richard, Viscount Bulkeley.

LLANDRYGARN *St Trygard* SH 383796

The nave walling may be 13th century but the collar-beam roof and the south doorway, round arched under a square frame, are late medieval. When a chancel was added in 1872 the original east window was reset in the west wall and the former north doorway was reset as a priest's doorway in the chancel south wall.

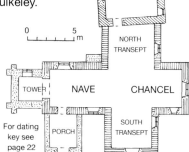

Plan of Llandegfan Church

Llandegfan Church

Llandyfrydog Church

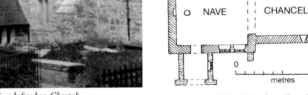

Plan of Llanddyfnan Church

Plan of Llandyfrydog Church

LLANDYFRYDOG St Dyfrydog   SH 444854

The almost square nave of c1400 has a chancel arch of that period, north and south windows of two lights, a south doorway with quarter-round mouldings and a blocked north doorway. The chancal was rebuilt about a hundred years later and has a three-light window with wave-moulded jambs and a four-centred head with beast stops.

LLANDYSILIO St Tysilio   SH 552717

This small 13th century single chamber with an octagonal font of that date lies on a small island near Thomas Telford's suspension bridge. The three pairs of roof crucks have braces forming almost semi-circular arches. None of the windows are ancient.

Llandysilio Church

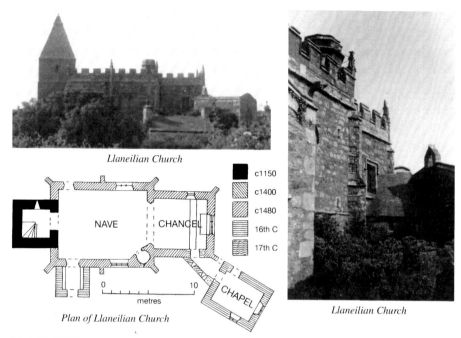

Llaneilian Church

c1150
c1400
c1480
16th C
17th C

Plan of Llaneilian Church

Llaneilian Church

LLANEDWEN   *St Edwen*   SH 517683

The existing church in the park of Plas Newydd is of 1854-6 but some of the roof timbers may be reused medieval work and there is a door-head remaining from a 15th century screen with a lion and wyvern on one side of the spandrels, backed against lions passant and a shield-bearing angel. There is a monument to Robert Hughes of Plas Coch, d1764.

LLANEILIAN   *St Eilian*   SH 470929

The 12th century west tower with two upper set-back stages and a stone pyramidal roof dates back to when a Celtic monastery existed here. Rebuilt under patronage from rector Nicholas ab Ellis, Archdeacon of Anglesey in 1474, and dated 1480 on a south buttress, the church has a nave with buttresses set diagonally at all four corners and in the middle each side and a narrower chancel also with diagonal corner buttresses and a three-light east window. The nave has three-light windows and original north and south doorways. Both parts are embattled with corner pinnacles. Contemporary with the church are the fine screen and roodloft and the choir stalls. The south porch may be early 16th century. Joined to the chancel SE corner by a passage dated 1614 is the almost square shrine chapel of St Eilian dating from c1400 and on a considerably different alignment from the rest of the church. Of the late 15th century are the cambered roof and plain parapets and the wooden shrine base inside.

LLANERCHYMEDD   *St Mary*   SH 418841

The long nave and chancel are of the 1850s but the lowest stage of the tower with a round arch towards the nave is probably 12th century, making it probable that there was once a Celtic monastery here.

LLANEUGRAD   *St Tysilio*   SH 495842

The tiny nave with a blocked south loop and the narrower chancel reached by a plain round arch are both 12th century. With them goes the tapered font with a band round the base. The chancel has an arch-braced 15th century roof, whilst the nave roof is 18th century. The whole of the chancel north wall was removed in the 16th century when a north chapel was added. It has an original roof with arch-braced trusses and a blocked west doorway. A carving of the Crucifixion set against a wheel-cross has come from over the south doorway. The exterior of the church is now all rendered.

LLANFACHRAETH   *St Machraeth*   SH 313831

The church had a good original east window until it was entirely rebuilt in 1878. Several items have survived, however, such as a recut font, part of a pew with the Bulkeley family arms, part of a 10th century wheel-cross with interlacing and a Crucifixion scene, and stones with human faces reset in the west wall.

LLANFAELOG   *St Maelog*   SH 337730

Only the late medieval doorway now in the vestry north wall survived the rebuilding of 1847. The 12th century font with chevrons and a Maltese cross has come from Talyllyn. A plaque commemorates Margaret Roberts, one of a party of people drowned in 1785 whilst crossing the Menai Strait.

LLANFAES   *St Catherine*   SH 604779

The church now looks Victorian although in fact the nave is 13th century, the chancel is 14th century and the west tower was added by Lord Bulkeley in 1811. Llanfaes was originally a town but in the 1290s it was suppressed to avoid competition with the new royal town at Beaumaris nearby, and the inhabitants moved to Newborough. There are fragments of 14th century grave-slabs with Lombardic inscriptions outside and also a slab with an indent of a brass of c1310 to an archdeacon of Anglesey. The oldest monuments inside the church are of Henry Whyte, d1728, and Jane Whyte, d1749.

Llanfaethlu Church

Llanfair Mathafarn Eithaf Church

LLANFAETHLU   *St Maethlu*   SH 313871

The church had a good original east window until entirely rebuilt in 1878. Several items have survived, however, a recut font, part of a pew with the Bulkeley family arms, part The long nave and south porch are early 15th century. Later plaster coved ceilings must hide original roofs. The east window was reset in a new chancel added in 1874. There is a brass to Rector William Griffith, d1587 and a monument to several 18th century members of the Griffith family. Other monuments are to Mary and William Vickers, he died in 1792, and Rice and Jane Jones, who both died in 1786.

LLANFAIR MATHAFARN EITHAF   *St Mary*   SH 507829

The nave and chancel are both early 15th century, the north doorway and west window being original. The round-arched south doorway is later. The porch in front of it and the other windows are of 1848. There is a state memorial to David, son of William Daniel, d1724. Of the 12th and 13th centuries are two grave covers with crosses, one having four circles as the cross-head. Outside is an 11th century extended-arm wheel-cross.

LLANFAIR YN Y CWMWD   *St Mary*   SH 447668

The plain single chamber has windows perhaps of the late 16th century. Inside are a 13th century coffin lid with tentrils around a cross and a 12th century font with a oval bowl with chevrons and crosses on a rectangular base with heads on the corners.

For dating key see page 22

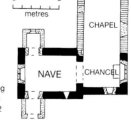

Plan of Llaneugrad Church

Llanfairynghornwy Church

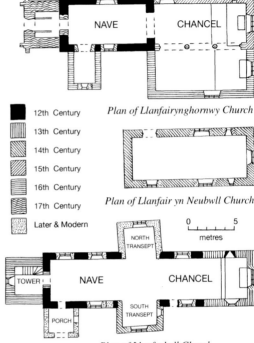

■ 12th Century
▨ 13th Century
▧ 14th Century
▨ 15th Century
▤ 16th Century
▦ 17th Century
▚ Later & Modern

Plan of Llanfairynghornwy Church

Plan of Llanfair yn Neubwll Church

Plan of Llanfechell Church

Llanfechell Church

LLANFAIRYNGHORNWY *St Mary*   SH 327908

The round chancel arch suggests the small nave is 12th century, although the doorway and two-light window on the south side are 14th century and the north window is typical 16th century work with three arched lights. A new chancel longer than the nave was added in the late 15th century. It had an arch-braced roof and a two-light east window. A chapel with a three-bay arcade of four-centred arches was added on the south side of the chancel in the early 16th century. A plan to add a north chapel in 1847 was never carried out. The west tower with an embattled parapet and small angle buttresses was added c1660. It now forms a porch and the south porch is now a vestry.

LLANFAIR YN NEUBWLL *St Mary*   SH 297778

The twin east lancets with an image light above, the trefoiled lancet on the south side and the north doorway suggest a date of c1300 for this single chamber with the trusses of the arch-braced roof sprung so low they resemble crucks. A 15th century north window has had its label moulding hacked off.

LLANFECHELL *St Mechell* SH 370913

The nave and the chancel both have 12th century south doorways with crudely made imposts and thin voussoirs and there is a contemporary square font with pairs of arches on each side. One original north window was moved further east when the chancel was lengthened in the 13th century. This may originally have been a monastic church with a small central tower. The existing west tower with three set-offs is 16th century. Within the massive parapet is a short octagonal stone spire of the 18th century set over a circular vault. The short transepts are 14th century, are is the main roof with close-set arch-braced trusses and the east window, The south transept arch has hollow chamfers, the north transept arch being a 19th century copy of it. The south porch contains a 13th century cross-slab with large floriations.

LLANFFLEWYN *St Figael* SH 350891

The single chamber was partly rebuilt in 1864. The sill of the east window is formed from a 14th century grave-slab. Also of that period is the roughly cut nine sided font.

LLANFIGAEL *St Fflewin* SH 328828

Rebuilding in 1841 followed a forty year period of ruination, yet the collar-beam trusses of the roof appear to be 18th century. Furnishings of the 1840s fill the interior. The only certain medieval feature is a 14th century octagonal font with filleted corners.

LLANFIHANGEL DIN SYLWY *St Michael* SH 588815

The octagonal font and the chancel and nave are all of c1400, but the latter was rebuilt in 1854. The east wall has a cross on the gabled finial and a three-light window with a hoodmould with a head and a stag for stops. There is a straight headed south window of two lights and a blocked priest's doorway. The arch-braced roof is probably original. Dating from 1628 is a pulpit composed of four sides of a hexagon carved with fretwork, foliage and dolphins.

Llanfihangel Din Sylwy Church

Doorway at Llanfair ym Neubwll

Monument at Llangadwalladr

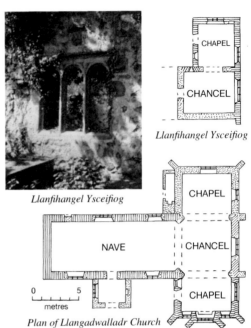

Llanfihangel Ysceifiog

Llanfihangel Ysceifiog

Plan of Llangadwalladr Church

LLANFIHANGEL TRE'R BEIRDD   *St Michael*   SH 459837

Features which survived rebuildings in 1811 and 1888 are a 14th century window and doorway, the latter with broaches at the foot of a continuous chamfer, the octagonal font, a 15th century cinquefoiled window in the chancel, grave-slabs with ring crosses at top, centre and bottom, and a 13th century incised cross with trefoiled arms.

LLANFIHANGEL YN NHOWYN   *St Michael*   SH 321774

Parts of the single chamber survived the rebuilding of 1862 but the only ancient feature is a recut font. A church of 1862 from LLanynghenedl was moved here in 1988 and now adjoins the original building to serve R.A.F. Valley.

LLANFIHANGEL YSGEIFIOG   *St Michael*   SH 478735

This ruin lies hidden away at the end of a long, leafy track. In c1850 the nave was demolished and the chancel west end walled up. The south wall is of the 1870s, when the south chapel was pulled down. The east window is early 16th century. The north chapel added by the Hollands of Plas Berw has an east window with a shield and the date 1598. Windows and a doorway appear to have been reused in the church of 1847 in the nearby village of Gaerwen which superseded the old church.

LLANFFINAN   *St Ffinan*   SH 496755

The church was rebuilt in 1844 but contains a 12th century font with interlacing.

LLANFWROG   *St Mwrog*   SH 302839

Only an octagonal font, possibly recut, survived the rebuilding of 1864.

LLANGADWALADR *St Cadwaladr* SH 384693

The only medieval features to have survived the rebuilding of 1857-9 are the blocked 13th century north doorway with roll-mouldings and the elliptical 15th century chancel arch. Reset in the Victorian east window is stained glass of the 1480s with angels St Mary and St John, and the donors Meuric ap Llywelyn of Bodowen and his wife Margoed. The glass seems to have commemorated the safe return of their son Owain (who is depicted with his wife Elen Meredith of Glenllifon) from Henry Tudor's victory over Richard III at Bosworth. The Meyrick Chapel north of the chancel is dated 1640 but was mostly rebuilt in 1811 and 1856. On the south side is the spectacular Bodowen Chapel added in 1659-61 by the ardent Royalist Colonel Hugh Owen and his wife Ann Williams of Llys Dulas, who are depicted kneeling towards each other in a monument over the chapel west doorway. The chapel has medieval-looking windows of two tiers of four trefoil-headed lights facing east and south, the latter window set in a projecting bay with its own diagonal corner buttresses like those of the main chapel. Smaller two-light windows are set between the two sets of buttresses.

LLANGAFFO *St Caffo* SH 350891

The church of 1846 is of little interest apart from its tower being a landmark across the Malltraeth Marsh. Older features are a recut 12th century font with a saltire pattern, the octagonal 17th century pulpit, pediments and cherubs from a wall-monument of c1660, an inscribed pillar (in the vestry), part of the head of a wheel-cross with interlace, and a selection of six cross-slabs of the 7th century through to the 11th century.

LLANGEFNI *St Cyngar* SH 458759

Only a doorway reset in the vestry and 12th century font now lying disused in the tower survived a rebuilding of 1824 for Viscount Bulkeley. A 5th century inscribed stone lies by the west doorway.

LLANGEINWEN *St Ceinwen* SH 440659

The plain blocked round-arched north doorway suggests the nave walling is 12th century, whilst the roof appears to be 14th century. The east end is a later addition but has no datable old features. The west tower and the windows are of 1829 and the north chapel was added in 1838. There are fleur-de-lys and palmettes in relief on the circular font with a roll-moulding on its base.

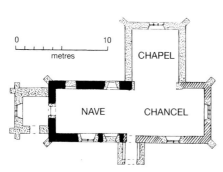

Plan of Llangeinwen Church   *Old doorway at Llangeinwen*

Llangristiolus Church

LLANGOED   *St Cawrdaf*   SH 611806

Survivals of the rebuilding of 1881 of the cruciform church are the north transept dated 1612 with a segmental headed doorway with a keystone, the reset 14th century east window of three lights (see photograph), the plain 14th century font, the tapered octagonal pulpit dated 1622, and part of a 13th century foliated cross-slab. There are 17th and 18th century slate memorials to members of the Hughes family.

LLANGRISTIOLUS   *St Cristiolus*   SH 450736

The font with six panels under sub-arches is 12th century and with it goes those parts of the nave that survived the rebuilding of 1852. A fine arch leads into the 13th century chancel, higher and wider than the nave, and also mostly rebuilt except for the east wall with a five-light early 16th century window. The porch may be late 16th century.

LLANGWYFAN   *St Cwyfan*   SH 336684

The churchyard is now a circular tidal island but in medieval times it was a promontory and the retaining wall is no older than the 1890s. Nowadays the church is frequented much more by tourists than worshippers. Some 12th century walling with a doorway and stone benching remains on the south side but the main body is otherwise 14th century work with a later doorway. The three blocked up four-centred arches opened into a 16th century north aisle demolished in the early 19th century, when the south porch was also removed. The arch-braced roof is partly 16th century. See page 34.

LLANGWYLLOG   *St Cwyllog*   SH 434798

The single chamber may be partly late 12th century, the period of the cable-moulded font. The north doorway and parts of the roof and the three-light east window are late 15th century. Several plain windows and the separate western chamber perhaps intended as a school room are late 16th century. The reading desk is dated 1769 and also of that date are the three-decker pulpit, the altar rails and the benches near them, and one of the two box pews. There are slate tablets to members of the Hughes family of Bryngola and the Pritchards of Trescawen.

Llanidan Church

Window at Llangoed

LLANIDAN   *St Nidan*   SH 495669

The original long narrow church was given a north aisle with a six bay arcade in the late 15th century. Most of the church was unroofed in 1844, when the 13th century font with interlaced fleur-de-llys and a later medieval reliquary found under the altar were taken off to the new church east of Brynsiencyn, but the western third survived in use as a mortuary chapel.

It has a 14th century south doorway to which a porch with a pointed barrel vault was later added. The arcade is intact but most of the outer walls of the eastern parts have now gone.

■ 12th Century
▦ 13th Century
▧ 14th Century
▨ 15th Century
▤ 16th Century
▒ Later & Modern

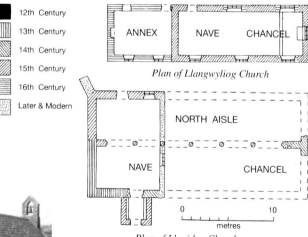

ANNEX   NAVE   CHANCEL

Plan of Llangwyliog Church

NORTH AISLE

NAVE   CHANCEL

0   10
metres

Plan of Llanidan Church

Llangwyllog Church

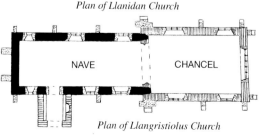

NAVE   CHANCEL

Plan of Llangristiolus Church

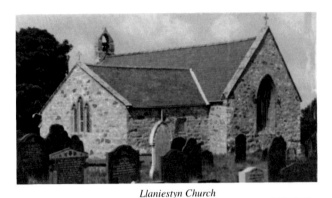

Llaniestyn Church

Doorway at Llaniestyn

Plan of Llangwyfan Church

Plan of Llanrhwydrys Church

- ■ 12th Century
- ▦ 13th Century
- ▨ 14th Century
- ▤ 16th Century
- ▒ Later & Modern

LLANIESTYN *St Iestyn* SH 585796

The 12th century font has blind arcading, chevrons, interlacing, spirals, chequers and a Maltese cross. The main chamber seems to be mostly late 14th century except perhaps for the blocked west doorway and the 16th century south doorway with its arch set within a moulded square frame. The south transept is a later addition. It contains a 14th century slab depicting St Iestyn as a bearded hermit with a cloak, broach, hood, staff, scroll and an inscription mentioning Wenllian ferch Madoc and her nephew Gruffudd ap Gwilym, d1405, from whom the Penrhyn family were descended.

LLANRHUDDLAD *St Rhuddlad* SH 305896

Only the font is medieval. The church itself was rebuilt on a new site in 1858.

LLANRHWYDRYS *St Rhwydrys* SH 322932

The small nave with its round arched doorway and the font with a base band are 12th century. A narrower but longer chancel with two pairs of cruck roof trusses was added in the 13th century, when the nave was also given a pair of cruck trusses. The chancel has original gable copings and the nave has a bellcote which may be 14th century. The early 15th century east window has panel tracery and hoodmould stops in the form of angels holding shields. The tiny north chapel may be 16th century and there is a west gallery dated 1776. The lychgate and the sanctuary celure are early 19th century.

LLANSADWRN *St Sadwrn* SH 554759

The church was much restored in 1881, when a north porch and new bellcote were provided. Original are the north doorway and the six arch-braced roof trusses whch are 15th century, and the 16th century roof trusses and gargoyles of a capped man and a bear on the north transept. The font is a classical style pillar dated 1737. On the chancel north wall is a small stone of c600 commemorating St Sadwrn and his wife. There are tablets to John Roberts, d1711, and Elizabeth Wynne, d1714.

LLANTRISANT

St Afran, St Ieuan & St Sannan   SH 349841

The font of c1200 has three rings around the rim and two below. The main body appears to be 14th century, the date of the two-light east window with a shield-shaped light above two trefoils. A large transept with 18th century roof trusses projects south from this end. There are monuments to John Wynn of Bodewryd, d1669, Hugo Williams of Nantanog, d1670, and the Reverend Morgan Ellis, d1789. The roof has been restored since part of it collapsed in 1968. The church is now merely an ancient monument, services being held in the new church of 1899 located 1.5km to the SE.

Llanrhydrys Church

LLANWENLLWYFO   *St Gwenllwyfo*   SH 485901

Following the collapse of the roof in 1950 plain walls now reduced to about 1.5m high are all that remain of this church. It was restored in the 18th century but later abandoned in favour of a new church 1km to the SW serving the village of Dulas. To the new church were taken the octagonal font and the brass depicting Marcelie Lloyd, d1607 and her husband Richard Williams with their three sons.

The new church also has a fine series of panels of early 16th century stained glass collected and presented by the Neave family. The glass in the east window came from the chapel of Pope Adrian VI of 1522 at the Carthusian monastery at Louvain. Adrian was tutor to the Emperor Charles V, whose head lies in the quatrefoil of the window.

LLECHGYNFARWY

St Cynfarwy   SH 381811

The church has a 12th century font with four saltire crosses and a Baroque monument to Helen Bold, d1631 in the south chapel, which is dated 1664 with initials of William Bold of Tre'r Ddol. Otherwise the building is mostly of the restoration of 1867.

Llanwenllfo Old Church

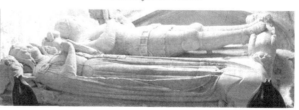

Effigies at Penmynydd

NEWBOROUGH *St Peter* SH 420655

Newborough was founded by Edward I to accommodate Welsh people transferred from Llanfaes, which was considered too close to the newly founded English garrison town of Beaumaris. Much of the church is early 14th century and the three-light east window has reticulated tracery. The nave was lengthened westwards and given a new south porch and double bellcote in the late 15th century. The extension may have replaced a tower mentioned in a 14th century poem. Walling older than the founding of the new town may lie hidden under the roughcasting of the nave and the church was originally dedicated to St Anno. It contains a 12th century font with an interlaced cross with knot patterns and Maltese cross and memorials to two 14th century priests, David Barker having a sandstone slab with palmettes radiating from a cross-head and Matheus ap Elye having an effigy in relief in a niche in the chancel south wall.

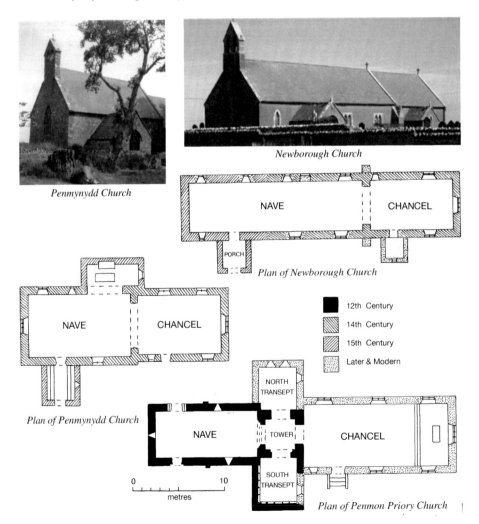

Penmynydd Church

Newborough Church

NAVE   CHANCEL

PORCH

Plan of Newborough Church

NAVE   CHANCEL

■ 12th Century

▨ 14th Century

▨ 15th Century

▦ Later & Modern

Plan of Penmynydd Church

NORTH TRANSEPT

NAVE   TOWER   CHANCEL

SOUTH TRANSEPT

0   10

metres

Plan of Penmon Priory Church

PENMON *St Seiriol* SH 630808

Dating of the various parts of the 12th century cruciform church has been subject to considerable debate. Recent work suggests that the central tower originally stood at the west end of a small nave within the western half of that is now a chancel of 1855 upon mid 13th century foundations, and that the existing nave and transepts at a higher level were added in the mid 12th century. The nave has an original south doorway, a pilaster on each of the north and south sides, and single small round-headed windows facing north, west and south. The south transept has five bays of blind arcading along the inside of its west and south walls. The east wall was rebuilt in 1855, when the north transept was entirely rebuilt. The tower has original small twin round-arched belfry windows facing north and east and is covered with a pyramidal stone roof. Delights within include a 10th or 11th century font, a bearded head and a sheila-na-gig in the south transept, a pillar piscina, and two 10th or 11th century crosses, one showing St Anthony tempted by demons, and the Flight into Egypt, with interlace and knotwork.

   In 1237 Llywelyn Fawr granted Penmon to the Celtic monastery 2.5km to the NW on Priestholm (Puffin Island) just across a narrow strait from Penmon and also confusingly dedicated to St Seiriol. The Priestholm community transferred to Penmon and was re-organised as a priory of Augustinian canons. They added a larger new chancel to the church and laid out a cloister 14m square south of it with a refectory and dormitory block on the south side (now a ruin in state care). Probably of late medieval date is the west range adjoining the south transept and obscuring its original south window.

PENMYNYDD *St Gredifael* SH 517750

The north chapel contains an alabaster tomb-chest with shields on the sides. It was transferred here in the 16th century from Llanfaes Friary and was probably made in the East Midlands. On it are fine late 15th century effigies of Gronw Fychan of Penmynydd, d1382 (ancestor of Henry VII) and his wife Myfanwy. They probably provided patronage for a rebuilding of the church, which has east and west windows of three lights and side-windows of two lights. The chancel is unusually wide and bears the Tudor arms and incorporates reset 12th century stones with chevrons outside. The priest's doorway and the windows have hollow chamfered rere-arches. The font is 15th century.

Penmon Priory: the south transept interior

Penmon Priory Church

Trefdraeth Church

Pentraeth Church

Plan of Talyllyn Church

PENRHOS LLIGWY   *St Michael*   SH 481859

A chancel of c1400 with a collarbeam-truss roof has been added to a
nave which was then given a similar roof which was subsequently rebuilt.

PENTRAETH   *St Mary*   SH 524785

Parts of the walls and the reset three-light east window are late 14th century, but the
east end (probably an extension) and the south porch date from the rebuilding of 1882.
Of c1600 are reset windows in the chancel north wall and the south chapel east wall.
Some roof trusses are also ancient. A barrel-shaped font is reset in the porch as a
stoup. The oldest monuments are those of John Jones of Plas Gwyn, Dean of Bangor,
d1727, William Jones, d1755, and the latter's daughter Jane Panton, d1764.

RHODOGEIDIO   *St Ceidio*   SH 411855 & 399855

Rebuilding in 1845 left just the 14th century east window, the 15th century font and the
round arched and hollow-chamfered north doorway which could be 17th century.
    The small church of St Mary out in the fields 1km to the west has an east window
and arch-braced roof trusses suggesting a 15th century date. The font is much older.

RHOSBERIO   *St Peirio*   SH 391918

The walls are ancient but no old features survive. The font may be 12th century.

RHOSCOLYN   *St Gwenfaen*   SH 268757

The only features to survive rebuilding in the 1870s were the 18th century memorials to
the Owens of Bodior, the late 15th century south doorway with a square outer frame,
and the font with fluting and saltire crosses on the octagonal bowl and tiny cusped
panels on the tapered base.

TALYLLYN   *St Mary or St Tudur*   SH 367728

The nave with its round-arched west doorway, stone benches and no south windows
may be 12th century. The chancel was partly rebuilt in the 16th century when it was
given a new three-light east window, but the chancel arch and one roof truss are older.
The nave also has two old roof trusses. A small 17th century chapel projects from the
east end of the chancel south wall. There is a 15th century font. The simple 18th century furnishings include altar-rails and backless benches.

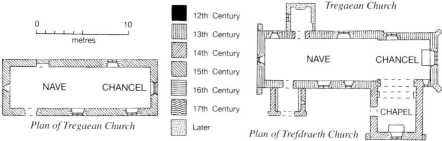

■	12th Century
▥	13th Century
▨	14th Century
▧	15th Century
▤	16th Century
▧	17th Century
░	Later

0   10
metres

NAVE   CHANCEL

Plan of Tregaean Church

Tregaean Church

NAVE   CHANCEL

CHAPEL

Plan of Trefdraeth Church

TREARDDUR   *St Bridget*   SH 256790

Until the late 18th century ruins of a small chapel stood on the mound of sand here.

TREFDRAETH   *St Beuno*   SH 408704

The 14th century bellcote and three-light east window with mouchettes in the flowing tracery are the earliest parts of the nave and chancel, which probably have 13th century walling. There is also a 12th century font with six panels, four of which contain saltire crosses and another a knotwork cross. A vestry of the 1850s covers the late 15th century north doorway. A chancel north window under a square label with stops is also of that period, to which may also belong the nave roof with close-set collar-trusses with every third one arch-braced and fragments of old glass in one south window. The altar rails and the porch roof are 18th century, although the porch itself seems older. There are memorials to Chancellor Robert Lewis of Bangor, d1766, and to Hugh Lewis, d1666 and Owern Williams of Marian, d1723.

TREGAEAN   *St Caean*   SH 451798

The east window dates the single chamber as late 14th century, although it contains a 12th century font with chevrons. The bellcote is slightly ogival shaped and has sub-gables on either side. The south doorway with a square outer frame is late 15th century. Several windows and the arch-braced trusses of the roof are early 17th century.

GAZETTEER OF CHURCHES IN CAERNARVON & MERIONETH

ABERDARON *St Hywyn* SH 174266

This was once the most important church in the Llyn peninsular, serving a Celtic monastery. There are two 5th to 6th century stones with inscriptions to the priests Varacius and Senacus. The north walls of the original 12th century nave survive with a good west doorway of three chamfered orders. The east end of this part is 14th century and has a 12th century priest's doorway reset on the north side and a restored three-light 15th century east window. The flat-topped west bellcote is 14th century. A new south nave with five bay arcade of four-centred arches was added c1500. It has a doorway and a pair of three-light windows facing south and a five-light east window with cusped ogival-heads below a transom. The plain font and stoup are also both late medieval.

ABERERCH *St Cawdaf* SH 395365

The nave may be 14th century in origin although it has a 15th century west doorway. It has a roof with arch-braced collars and cusped struts. The east end and its roof is 15th century. It was given a large new five-light east window c1520, when the original three-light window was reset in the east wall of a chapel added on the north side. The chapel was soon extended westwards to make an aisle and the arcade is divided into two sections of two four-centred arches with a short central section of wall between them with slots for former screens. The aisle also has an original roof. The font is old and

and there are late medieval stalls with winded heads on the hand rests and water-lilies and roses on the four misericords. There is a 13th century graveslab with a shield, sword and spear in the sanctuary.

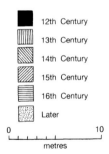

■	12th Century
▨	13th Century
▧	14th Century
▨	15th Century
▤	16th Century
▒	Later

0 _____ 10
metres

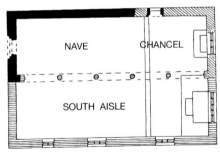

Plan of Aberdaron Church

Interior of Aberdaron Church

Aberffraw Church

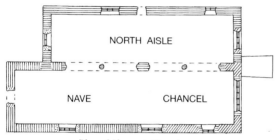

Plan of Abererch Church

Aberdaron Church

ABERGWYNGREGYN   *St Bodfan*   SH 653727

The church was rebuilt in 1878 but contains monuments to Mary Hughes, d1741, John Hughes, d1752, Sir Thomas Bond, d1734 and his wife Dorothy, d1738, the Reverend Williams Griffith, d1773, Richard Jones, d1720 and Lumley Owen d1784, the Reverend Richard Owen, d1788 and his wife, and the naval officer John Crawley, d1815.

BEDDGELERT   *St Mary*   SH 591480

The small Augustinian priory here was badly damaged by fire c1282, and again in c1432, but survived until 1536, when it had three canons and nine "religious men". The priory buildings probably lay beyond the rebuilt south wall of the church. The chancel with a good set of triple east lancets and the finely detailed two bay arcade on the north side of the nave are 13th century. The arcade now opens into a chapel of c1880 which replaced a lost full length aisle. The western part of the nave north wall and the west wall probably remain from the 12th century church of the original Celtic monastery. There is a monument to Evan Lloyd of Hafod Lwyfog, d1678.

BETWS GARMON   *St Garmon*   SH 551562

The church of 1841 contains a font dated 1614 and a monument to John Rowlands of Nant, 1703, brought here from the medieval church, which lay further to the east.

Beddgelert Church

BETWS-Y-COED   *St Michael*   SH 796566

Superseded by an impressive and more centrally placed new church of 1872, the old church lies down a lane towards the river. The fine effigy of Dafydd ap Gruffydd Goch, c1385 in armour once lay in the recess in the chancel north wall. The south doorway may also be 14th century and the square font with segmental arches with leaf patterns is of c1200. The old roof is hidden behind a plaster vault. The north chapel was added by Lord Willoughby de Eresby in 1843. The double-decker pulpit and reading desk have old parts including early 16th century linenfold panels, possibly from Gwydir Castle. Fragments of 16th century Dutch stained glass remain in the east window.

BODUAN   *St Buan*   SH 325377

The cruciform Georgian church of 1765 was much altered in 1894 when the nave was extended westwards and a tower added over the crossing. The earliest of the Wynn family monuments are those of Griffith, d1680, Sir William, d1754, Sir John, d1773.

BRYNCROES   *St Mary*   SH 228314

The lower parts of the walls and the font formed from a hollowed out boulder are probably medieval. The round-arched west and north doorways and the arch-braced roof trusses are late 16th century. There are late 17th century framed oak boards commemorating members of the Trygarn family.

CAERHUN   *St Mary*   SH 777708

The original triple east lancets have been reset in the east wall of a 15th century extension. The nave has 18th century north windows but retains some old roof trusses and contains an early font, next to which is a 16th century stoup. The much rebuilt south porch (now a vestry) and the west wall with its arched doorway are late medieval. The double bellcote is set on four corbels with a crucifix above the middle, and is flat-topped but with a tiny gablet facing west. Edward Williams of Maes-y-castell added the south chapel in 1591, re-using older windows and a 13th century corbel with heads perhaps from Aberconwy Abbey. The monuments nclude those of Hugh Davies of Caerhun, d1721, and Katherine Roberts, d1739.

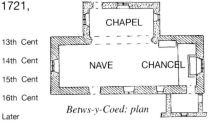

Betws-y-Coed: plan

13th Cent
14th Cent
15th Cent
16th Cent
Later

Betws-y-Coed Church

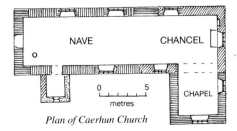

0   5
metres

Plan of Caerhun Church

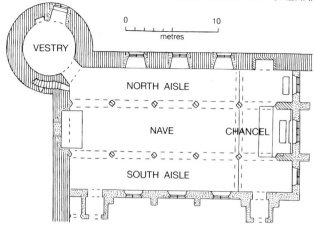

Plan of Caernarfon Church

Caerhun Church

CAERNARFON   *St Mary*   SH 477629

In 1307 the people of the newly built walled town were provided with a chapel-of-ease to Llanbeblig. The chapel was tucked into the NW corner so that the town wall formed the north and west sides, with the lowest level of the circular corner tower providing a vestry and the room above accommodating the chaplain. The thinner east and south walls were rebuilt in 1811 when three deep window embrasures were opened out through the north wall. Original are the five bay arcades carried on square chamfered-cornered piers set diagonally and similar arches dividing off the chancel and chapels.

Caernarfon Church

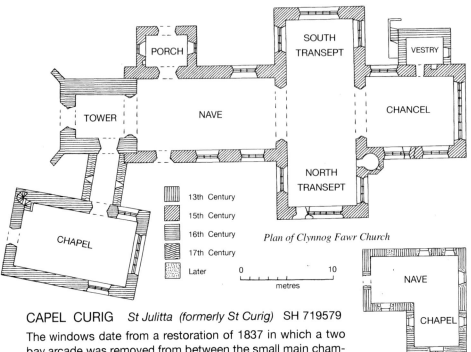

13th Century
15th Century
16th Century
17th Century
Later

0   metres   10

Plan of Clynnog Fawr Church

Capel Curig Church: plan

CAPEL CURIG *St Julitta (formerly St Curig)* SH 719579

The windows date from a restoration of 1837 in which a two bay arcade was removed from between the small main chamber, perhaps 13th century, and the chapel of c1500 beside the eastern half of the south side. A blocked NW doorway with a big lintel is the only original feature. The pulpit, reading desk and box pews are all of the 1830s.

Clynnog Fawr Church

CLYNNOG FAWR   *St Bueno*   SH 415497

The original Celtic monastery of St Beuno was succeeded by a college of priests and in the 1480s works began (at the east end) on rebuilding the church on a magnificent scale, making it the premier late medieval church in Gwynedd. It is all-embattled, with the parapets hiding very low-pitched roofs on all parts (only the nave roof with hammerbeams is original). A diagonally buttressed tower was added at the west end in the early 16th century. A wide central transept without north and south arches for a central crossing is divided by moulded arches from a two bay chancel and a three bay nave. The nave west bay has doorways on either side with a porch facing north, and the tower has a west doorway set under a square outer frame with bishop headstops and shields and tracery in the spandrels. The chancel has a priest's doorway and three ogival-headed sedilia and a piscina on the south side, and a three storey early 16th century vestry block on the north side. There are three-light windows in the side walls of the nave, transept and chancel. The transept end windows are of five lights and the east window has seven lights with panel tracery and sub-arches over the outer groups of three lights. There are cusped ogival heads on the second, fourth and sixth of the main lights. A polygonal SE turret contains a staircase to a roodloft over the screen.

A slab roofed passage connects a doorway on the south side of the tower with the north doorway of a large and formerly detached early 16th century chantry chapel set at an angle to the main church over the site of St Beuno's grave. The chapel also has a west doorway and windows of three lights facing north and south and of five lights facing east. Foundations of older structures were found under the floor here in 1913.

The chancel screen is dated 1531 and is surmounted by a loft of 1940. The tower arch screen is late 17th century. There are serpent motifs on four of the six sides of the pulpit of c1700. The late medieval font has a wooden bowl with trefoils on the sides. In the chancel are fourteen early 16th century choir stalls with misericords with vine-leaf and vaulting patterns. An incised Latin cross on a boulder may be 8th century and outside there is an Irish type granite sundial of the 12th century or possibly earlier.

The monuments include a table tomb and tablet to William Glyn, d1609, a brass in the north transept to two-year old William Glynne of Lleuar, d1633, an armorial slab to William Wynne, d1660, an altar tomb to George Twisleton, d1667, and a tablet to George Twisleton, d1714.

Chantry chapel at Clynnog Fawr Church

Interior of Clynnog Fawr Church

CONWY   *St Mary*   SH 781775

Cistercian monks from Strata Florida settled here c1188 and set up an abbey known as Aberconwy. Llywelyn Fawr was the main patron, he and three of his family being buried within the church, which was damaged in 1245 by an English raid. In 1277 the abbey was the place where Llywelyn ap Gruffudd was forced to sign a humiliating treaty with Edward I of England. The church was damaged in the English invasion of 1283 and later that same year the monks were transferred 12km southwards up the River Conwy to a new site at Maenan so that their original church could become the parish church of St Mary of the walled town then being begun around it.

Conwy parish church is now mostly a 14th century building consisting of a west tower, north and south aisles with arcades of three bays, a south transept and a chancel as wide at the nave with a small chapel on the north side of it, beyond which is a vestry of 1925. The transept has two good east windows, one with reticulated tracery and the other with intersecting tracery, but the south window is of the 1870s. The tower and the 17th century vestry north of it have been built against the original west wall of the nave and north aisle of the abbey. It has triple lancets over a fine doorway without fittings for a door which might be the chapter house entrance reset. Other possible remnants of the abbey church are the two tomb recesses in the south aisle and the lower parts of the east wall of the chancel, although its thickness is more typical for a parish church than a monastic one. The two 13th century windows in the chancel south wall must be reset as the original layout is likely to have had transepts slightly further east than the existing 14th century south transept. There is no evidence that a 14th century north transept ever existed. Late medieval features are the east window, the upper stage of the tower, the screen bearing the badge of Sir Richard Pole, the font with a buttressed base and tracery, and the choir stalls.

Conwy Church

In the chancel at Conwy Church are monuments to Dorothy Wynn, d1586, Robert Wynn, d1596, Edward Williams, d1601, Reverend John Brickdall, d1607, John Wynn, d1637, Margaret Coytmor, d1684, Jane Fletcher, d1708, Cadwaleder Wynn, d1752, Anne Apthorpe, d1788, The south transept contains monuments to Edward Holland, d1584, Johannes Hooke, d1600, Robert Williams, d1760 and Robert Howard, d1776. In the nave and aisles are monuments to Maria Williams, d1585 and John Williams, d1706 and a 14th century floriated cross-slab.

CRICCIETH   *St Catherine*   SH 500382

The north nave is a 15th century addition to the south nave, which is probably of 1230 at the west end and of c1300 at the east end. The arcade between the naves had just two arches until rebuilt in 1870s, when the roof was altered and most of the windows renewed. There is a modern extension on the north side. The oak reredos is dated 1679, and the altar-rails are late 18th century.

DOLBENMAEN   *St Mary*   SH 507433

Although the openings have all been restored, the small 15th century single chamber has an original roof with cusped kingposts, purlins in pairs and exposed rafters.

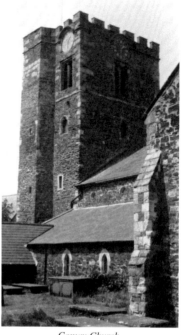

Conwy Church

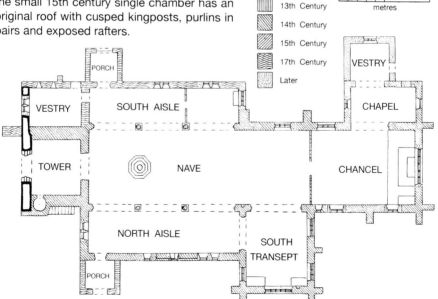

Plan of Conwy Church

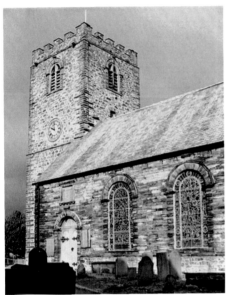

Dolgellau Church

Gwydir Uchaf Chapal

DOLGELLAU   *St Mary*   SH 727178

As rebuilt in 1716-23 the church comprises an aisled nave with arcades on oak beams supporting a cambered ceiling and an apsidal chancel. A west tower was added in 1727. The large and round-arched windows have keystones only on the north side. The apse windows were altered in 1864 and an additional central window added in 1901, whilst the NE vestry is of c1830. There is a small font of 1651 in addition to one of 1861. The effigy of the mid 14th century knight Meuric ap Vychan with an inscription on his shield once lay in a side chapel which was removed during the rebuilding. Other monuments include those of Ludovicius Nanney, d1708, Jane Wynn, d1726, Robert Nanney, d1751, Lewis Nanney, d1779,

DOLWYDDELAN   *St Mary*   SH 781775

The small single chamber was rebuilt by Maredudd ap Ieuan, who took a lease on the estate in 1489 and was commemorated by a small brass figure in armour. The roof is original and has arch-braced trusses and a celure of ribs and bosses over the east end. There is also a contemporary screen and a slightly later font. There is a monument to the Wynn family and it was Robert Wynn of Plas Mawr, Conwy, who added the south transept c1590 with an arcade of two segmental arches on a monolithic Doric column. One north window has a stained glass figure of St Christopher. The pulpit is dated 1711 and with it go the reading desk and altar rails.

DWYGYFYLCHI   *St Gwynin*   SH 737773

The church was entirely rebuilt in 1760 (see the slate commemorative slab now in the vestry) and was mostly rebuilt again in 1889 using the 18th century walling. It contains a tablet to Rhys Lloyd, d1710 and tablets to the Smiths of Pendyffryn. There is a late medieval window-head reset near the SW corner of the building.

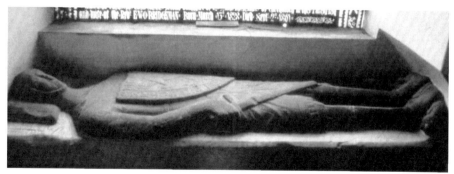

Effigy of a knight in Dolgellau Church

EDERN   *St Edern*   SH 274369

The cruciform church is now mostly a rebuilding of 1868 on the old foundations. The nave roof may be partly of c1400, and of c1500 are roof timbers in the transepts with decorative motifs underneath including bosses.

EGLWYSBACH   *St Martin*   SH 803706

Two west windows with arched lights look earlier than the rebuilding of 1782. A porch was added in 1837 and alterations were made in the 1880s. The tub font may be 12th century although it is dated 1731. The altar-rails may also pre-date 1782.

EGLWYS-YN-RHOS   *St Hilary*   SH 794804

The north transept has a 14th century two light west window with both the trefoiled heads cut from one stone. The nave is perhaps 13th century, like the goblet-shaped font, but now has only 19th century features apart from some parts of the roof of c1500. An older font with chevrons lies loose by the pulpit. There are monuments to members of the Mostyn family and a stone with a 5th or 6th century inscription.

GWYDIR UCHAF   *Holy Trinity*   SH 794609

This private manorial chapel was built by Sir Richard Wynn, whose initials and the date 1673 appear on a shield over the only doorway on the north side. The four-light east window and the three-light south windows have wooden frames and mullions. The painted ceiling betrays Sir Richard's Catholic sympathies and shows the Trinity, Creation, and a Last Judgement. Original fittings include a west gallery, a pulpit, the pews and altar rails.

GYFFIN   *St Benedict*   SH 776770

The eastern half of the nave and the narrower chancel represent the 13th century church. Until the restoration of 1866 the chancel retained a good 13th century doorway of three orders and surviving features of that period are the goblet-shaped font with fleur-de-lys and the coffin-lids in the porch. The roofs of close-set collar-trusses with painted panels at the east end are of c1500 when the nave was lengthened and given a new doorway still retaining its original door. A datestone of 1694 lies below the 19th century bellcote. The 16th century south chapel also has an old roof. The 17th century north chapel with its three bay arcade was rebuilt to provide a vestry in the 1860s. The altar-rails are mid 17th century.

LLANABER   *St Bodfan* & *St Mary*   SH 599181

The church lies on a slope above the sea and the high altar is reached by many steps up from the nave. Despite renewal of most of the windows it is the best preserved 13th century parish church in North Wales. The chancel probably lies on the site of the original 6th or 7th century chapel of St Bodfan. Each of the three bays has a lancet on each side and then the east bay has a two light window on the south side and an east lancet with an original three-rolled rere-arch. This bay has a panelled celure; the other bays have arch-braced trusses with cusped struts at the apex.

The nave has narrow aisles with five bays of chamfered arches with filleted outer rolls set on circular piers with foliage capitals mostly featuring downward-turned fleur-de-lys. Diamond-shaped leaves appear on the west responds and upright acanthus leaves on the NE respond. Above is a clerestory of plain lancets and a roof of tie-beams with curved struts and collars alternating with arch-braced collar-trusses. The fine south doorway has four orders each with triple shafts, the middle one pointed, and with fleur-de-lys capitals. The south porch of 1859 replaced a more massive 17th century structure with a bellcote like that at Llangelynin.

Two pillars with late 5th or early 6th century inscriptions lie in the north aisle. The chancel screen retails some old parts and there is a fine octagonal 14th century font with motifs such as a rose, a face, a plant, quatrefoils and a gargoyle face.

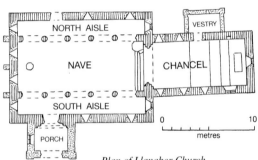

Plan of Llanaber Church

Llanaber Church

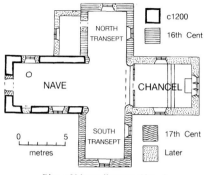

c1200
16th Cent
17th Cent
Later

Plan of Llanaelhaearn Church

Capitals on the south doorway at Llanaber

LLANAELHAEARN   *St Aelhaearn*   SH 388448

Now full of box-pews of c1800, the nave has a blocked doorway of c1200 on the south side and a west doorway probably of the 15th century. The 16th century north chapel retains an original two-light east window and has built into it a 6th century inscribed pillar. Another early pillar with an incised cross lies outside the west doorway. The south chapel is dated 1622 and has windows of windows with pairs of elliptical-headed lights. There is a similar window in the nave. The chapels only became transepts when a new chancel was added in 1892 to make the church properly cruciform. The original east window of three round-headed lights of equal height was then reused, as was the 16th century screen. There is a monument to Catherine Glyn of Elernion, d1702.

LLANARMON   *St Garmon*   SH 424394

Original east and SE windows remain in a new south nave added c1500 with a four bay arcade of four-centred arches of two hollow-chamfered orders on octagonal piers. The western part of the north nave may go back to the 12th or 13th century. This part has a an early 16th century screen and a late 16th century east window. The other windows, roofs and porch are of 1858-62. The font is 15th century. There are several slate tablets of the late 17th and 18th centuries, and a 17th century collecting box.

Llanaelhaearn Church

Llanbeblig Church

LLANBEBLIG *St Peblig* SH 487623

The church lies beside the site of the former Roman font of Segontium and is the original parish church of Caernarfon. The nave south wall goes back to when Llywelyn ap Gruffydd granted the church to Aberconwy Abbey and under this wall in 1894 was found a Roman altar. The chancel and transepts are late 14th century. The north transept was partly rebuilt in 1775 to contain a gallery (now removed) and the diagonally buttressed south transept has a good early 15th century window of five lights with a tomb recess and an ogival-headed piscina below it. The roof here seems to have once had a celure. The chancel was given new windows and battlements in the late 15th century. The nave north wall and roof and the west tower with a SW corner staircase are 15th century. The tower upper stage with stepped battlements is early 16th century. Some 16th century woodwork remains in the north porch.

The Vaynol Chapel on the north side was provided to contain the tomb of William Griffith and his wife whose arms and the date 1593 appear on the four-light east window. However there may have been an older chapel here as both the roof and the arch to the chancel look older. Reset in the chapel north wall is a good 14th century window. Above the chapel west doorway is a relief of what looks like a 14th century knight in a surcoat. Other monuments in the chapel are to Margaret Jones, d1716, Frances Rowlands, d1718, Captain John Lloyd, d1741, William Williams d1769. The chancel contains memorials to Lewis Meyrick, d1690, Richard Rowland, d1719, Margaret Oliver, d1796 and a rare brass with a tiny figure of the notary Richard Foxwist, d1500, lying in a bed holding a shield with the Five Wounds of Christ. In the transepts are memorials to William Bold, d1609 and Margaret Griffiths, d1784, and the nave contains two medieval coffin-lids with crosses on them and other similar fragments.

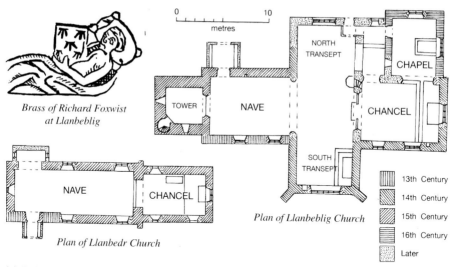

Brass of Richard Foxwist
at Llanbeblig

0   10
metres

NORTH TRANSEPT

CHAPEL

TOWER   NAVE

CHANCEL

SOUTH TRANSEPT

Plan of Llanbeblig Church

	13th Century
	14th Century
	15th Century
	16th Century
	Later

NAVE   CHANCEL

Plan of Llanbedr Church

LLANBEDR   *St Peter*   SH 586270

Of the church mentioned in the 13th century just a short section of thicker walling remains on either side of the south doorway. Otherwise the nave and chancel are mostly late medieval but apart from a few old roof timbers the features are mostly of 1883. The font and the roughly-made chancel arch may be 16th or 17th century. A granite boulder has spirals incised upon it, probably from the Neolithic period.

LLANBEDR-Y-CENNIN   *St Peter*   SH 760695

The south doorway and the tub font may be early 13th century. The single chamber was reroofed, lengthened eastwards and given a corbelled bellcote with a small relief of the Crucifixion in the 15th century. The porch and the north chapel with original roofs are 16th century. The chapel has one old timber-framed window. All the other windows are of 1842. There are altar rails of c1700 with 18th century box pews beside them. The two decker pulpit is dated 1724.

Llanbedr-y-Cennin Church

Llanbedr Church

LLANBEDROG   *St Patrick*   SH 329315

The nave may be 13th century. The chancel with a good original screen is 16th century, whilst the cusped recess outside the east wall may be older work reset. Also early 16th century is the octagonal font with quatrefoils, crosses, fleur-de-lys, a sunk lancet, and a Tudor window pattern, and also some stained glass with heads and a trumpeting angel in the west window. The oldest monument is to Anne Parry, d1730.

LLANDANWG   *St Tanwg*   SH 569283

Isolated on sand dunes south of Harlech, this was originally the parish church of the town. It was abandoned in favour of a new church in the town which now contains the font of c1500, but was restored c1900 by the Society for the Protection of Ancient Buildings. The western part has a doorway with a voussoired head, probably 13th century, whilst the eastern part is late 14th century and has a tall east window, the upper part of which was blocked up in the 17th century. Over the west doorway is a datestone of 1685. Just the top beam remains of the chancel screen. At the east end are a pillar and two stones with 5th or 6th century carvings on them.

LLANDDEINIOLEN   *St Deiniol*   SH 546659

The church is now of 1843 but contains a font dated 1665 with initials WS and WP plus monuments to Elizabeth and Jane, d1688, daughter and wife of Rector Robert Wynne, d1720, whose own plaque lies above, and William Thomas of Coed Helen, d1763.

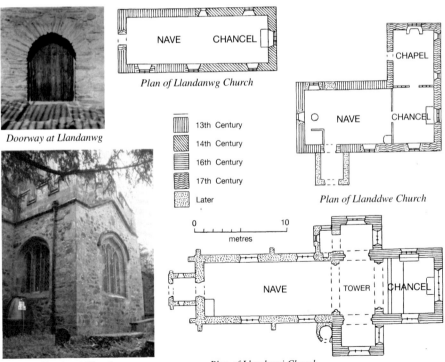

Doorway at Llandanwg

Plan of Llandanwg Church

13th Century
14th Century
16th Century
17th Century
Later

Plan of Llanddwe Church

0   10
metres

Llandegai Church

Plan of Llandegai Church

Llanddoged Church

LLANDDOGED   *St Doged*   SH 807635

The arcade of six plastered arches on timber posts between the two naves and most of the furnishings date from a rebuilding of 1838. Both parts have 16th century east windows with three arched lights and some other windows of stone may also be of that period. The font is old and 17th century panelling remains in the sanctuary. There are monuments to Sir Thomas Kyffin, 1752, and his later namesake, d1784.

LLANDDWYWE   *St Mary*   SH 587224

The blocked north doorway with a pointed voussoired head suggests a 13th century date for the nave. The chancel south wall was rebuilt in 1663 but contains windows of 1853. Also of the latter date is the porch, despite the datestone of 1593 upon it. The chancel north wall was replaced by a fine screen after the Vaughans of Corycedol added a chapel there in 1615 and probably also replaced the chancel east wall. The roof of arch-braced collar-trusses and with a celure with ribs and bosses at east end is 16th century. Late 17th century altar rails have been reused to close off the chancel. The lower part of the 18th century reredos reuses material from older stalls.

The Vaughan chapel contains monuments to Griffith, d1616 with his wife Katherine and children, Richard, d1734, Margaret, d1758, William, d1775, and Evan Lloyd, 1791. Their servant Elizabeth Jones, d1751 had a memorial outside the north wall.

LLANDECWYN   *St Tecwyn*   SH 633375

Only a recess in the chancel south wall survived the rebuilding of 1879. An inscribed stone mentioning the deacon Heli may be 11th century.

LLANDEGAI   *St Tegai*   SH 601710

A new chancel and transepts were added in the early 16th century to what was perhaps a late 14th century nave. The latter was mostly rebuilt and lengthened in 1853, when the parapets of the other parts were rebuilt and a new tower raised over the crossing. A west porch and a north vestry were also added. There are tombs with effigies of Sir William Griffith, d1506 and his wife, and John Williams, Archbishop of York, d1650, who was then owner of the adjoining Penrhyn estate.

The old church of St Tudno at Llandudno

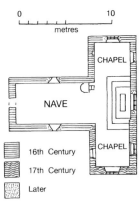

Plan of Llandudwen Church

LLANDUDNO   *St Tudno*   SH 769838

The church lies up on the Great Orme, far above the modern town. The plain pointed north and west doorways could be 13th century and there is a font of c1200 with billets and foliage. Two graveslabs with incised crosses of that period also remain. The east end and the arch-braced roof of eight bays with a moulded wall-plate in the chancel are late medieval. Just one beam with a vine trail remains from the chancel screen. The north porch has a 16th century roof and a room adjoins its eastern side.

LLANDUDWEN   *St Tudwen*   SH 274368

The main chamber and the north chapel are of the 1590s and the south chapel was added in the early 17th century to make a T-plan. The west doorway is off-centre. The south chapel windows have ovolo-moulded jambs and mullions. The chapels contain ledger stones to members of the Griffiths family of Nyffryn from 1670 to the 1770s.

Llandudwen Church

LLANDWROG   *St Twrog*   SH 451561

The ornate cruciform church is entirely of 1858-64. A font of 1703 lies in the porch. In the Glynllifon Chapel are some fine monuments, including those of Lady Frances Glyn, d1709 and Ellen Glyn, d1711, Thomas Wynn, d1749 and Frances Wynn, d1749, whilst the nave has a mid 18th century monument to the Bodvels of Bodfan.

LLANDYGWNNING   *St Gwyninin & St Tegonwy*   SH 266301

The church was rebuilt and refurnished in 1840. The pews incorporate 18th century panelling and the gallery balustrade re-uses older altar rails. The circular font with roll mouldings on the bowl and a seven-sided base may be 14th century. There are memorials to Elizabeth Williams, d1710, Jane Jones, d1721, and Margaret Williams, d1727,

LLANEGRYN   *St Mary & St Egryn*   SH 596058

The church belonged to Cymer Abbey and is mentioned in 1253. It has a square scalloped 12th century font with some old wooden panels around it However the main interest lies in the roofs of the main body and the south porch and in the very fine chancel screen of c1520 with panelled coving with big bosses supporting a roodloft

with tracery panels between buttresses. Bosses on the east side of the loft have motifs such as a stag and a serpent of eternity. The loft is now reached from a vestry on the north side and may originally have been accessed from outside. There are monuments to Richard Owen, d1714, Lewis Owen, d1729, and Edward Williams, d1763 and his wife, d1765.

Llanegryn Church

Roodloft at Llanegryn Church

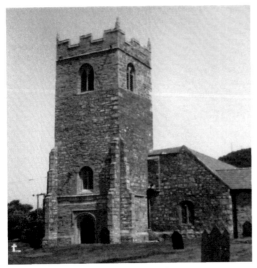

Llanengan Church

Llanelltyd Church

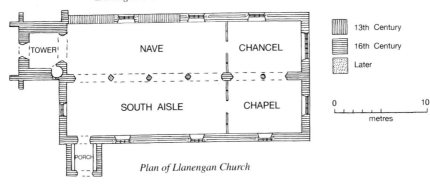

Plan of Llanengan Church

LLANELLTYD   *St Illtyd*   SH 717195

The north and south doorways with segmental-pointed heads are 13th or 14th century and the south porch is 16th century with an original roof, whilst the main body has an early 15th century roof of arch-braced collar-trusses. The north wall bears the date 1686 and there are two 18th century dormer windows on the south side. The bellcote is dated 1834 and the arched windows and north porch go with it. The older of two fonts is of 1689, and the pulpit has panels of 1692 and others which are medieval. There is a tablet to Sir Robert Vaughan, d1792. A 9th or 10th century inscription records the departure from here of a pilgrim called Kenyric or Reuhic.

LLANENDDWYN   *St Eddwyn*   SH 584234

The nave may retain some 13th century walling on the south side. The chancel is later and the transepts are 16th century, although the northern one was mostly rebuilt in 1883. Parts of the chancel and south transept roofs are 16th century and probably also the windows each with a semi-circular hood over two lancets in the nave and the south transept west wall. The octagonal font is probably late 15th century.

LLANENGAN   *St Engan*   SH 294270

The north nave north wall and roof trusses may go back to the 13th century. This nave was lengthened c1520 to create a chancel a painted celure of that period. Shortly afterwards a south nave was added with four bays of arches on lozenge-shaped piers towards the old nave and a further two arches (the east one later shortened) between the two chancels. Each chancel has an original screen of that period, with a loft on the southern one. The loft has openwork panels featuring a coiled snake, a tree and the Instruments of the Passion. There are old stalls on the east side of each screen. A richly moulded tower arch leads into a tower dated 1534 set at the west end of the old nave. There are late 17th century altar-rails and a late medieval font with quatrefoil and tracery patterns on the octagonal bowl and rosettes on the stem.

LLANFACHRETH   *St Machreth*   SH 755225

The church was entirely rebuilt in 1872-3 except for the tower and spire of 1820-22. The oldest monument is to Anne Nanney, d1729,

LLANFAELRHYS   *St Maelrhys*   SH 223278

Thinner walls mark out the eastern extension as later. The older part has blocked up north and south doorways with voussoired heads. The octagonal 15th century font has a cross incised on one side. The windows are all 19th century.

LLANFAGLAN   *St Baglan*   SH 455606

The main body is probably 13th century but the east end was rebuilt c1800, when a north porch was added. The south chapel is early 16th century. There are 18th century open benches, box pews and minor slate memorials. A 6th century inscribed pillar-stone is set over the doorway. Services are now held in a church of 1871 elsewhere.

LLANFAIR   *St Mary*   SH 577281

The east end with a three light window and the octagonal font are early 15th century. The later western end was rebuilt and given buttresses in 1858, when a ruined north chapel was replaced by a small vestry. The screen contains work of various periods. See picture on back cover.

LLANFAIRFECHAN   *St Mary*   SH 685744

The existing church is of 1849 and 1875. It contains memorials to John Roberts, d1728, and Catherine and Dorothy Roberts, d1763 and 1767.

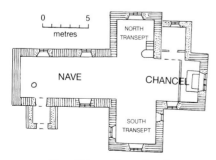

Plan of Llanenddwyn Church

Llanfaglan Church

Llanfair-is-Gaer Church

Llanfrothen Church

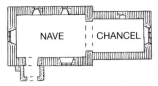

Plan of Llanfair-is-Gaer Church

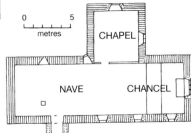

Plan of Llanfihangel-y-Pennant Church

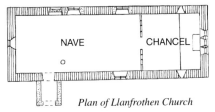

Plan of Llanfrothen Church

LLANFAIR-IS-GAER   *St Mary*   SH 501660

The bellcote appears to be 14th century but the walls of both the small nave and chancel are likely to be 13th century. The roofs are 17th or 18th century. The late medieval octagonal font has an incised floral disk and two raised motifs, a Gothic niche and a circled triskele. The 4s are set backwards on a datestone of 1644 with the initials RD and LL. Of c1600 is the stone with arms of Sir John Wynn of Gwydir. There are monuments to Catherine, daughter of Hugh Morgans of Rustrad, d1733 and to several 18th century members of the Wynn family of Llanfair.

LLANFIHANGEL BACHELLAETH   *St Michael*   SH 305342

This single chamber (now used as a house) may be 17th century. The bellcote and external steps to the west gallery plus the lancets along the sides are of 1847.

LLANFIHANGEL-Y-PENNANT   *St Michael*   SH 672088

The foundations of a single chamber with unmortared walls high up on the upper slope of Fridd Ty'n y Fach are said to be the remains of the original church of this district. From it came the 12th century scalloped font now in the existing church, which is mentioned in 1253 and was probably built by Llywelyn Fawr when Castell Y Bere was under construction in the 1220s, but lacks ancient features. The church was mostly rebuilt in the early 16th century when a north chapel was added. This retains its old roof and may have been used as a school-room in the 18th century. The nave west end has 17th century panelling. There is a monument to Anne Owen, d1724.

LLANFIHANGEL-Y-TRAETHAU   *St Michael*   SH 595354

The chief item of interest is the pillar west of the porch with an inscription probably of the 12th century referring to the "tomb of Wleder, mother of Odeleu, who first built this church in the time of King Owain". The east end of the single chamber is a later extension. The features are now essentially of 1845 and 1866 (when the vestry and bellcote were added, and 1884. There is a monument to John Owen, d1690.

LLANFOR   *St Mor*   SH 938368

The old church with a tower with crowstepped gables was replaced by a new one of 1874. The screen incorporates two medieval beams and a 13th century octagonal font lies outside. The tower contains a 6th century inscribed stone, dedication stones of 1599 from a former family chapel and monuments to Lady Sarah Bulkeley, d1714 and her son, Helena Langford of the same period, Robert Price, d1729 and his wife, d1748, William and Elizabeth Price, d1774 and 1778, and other Price memorials.

LLANFROTHEN   *St Brothen*   SH 622413

The two doorways, triple east lancets and single west lancet of the single chamber are all original 13th century work. The roof has 15th century timbers covered in thick old slates. Also late medieval are the octagonal font and the chancel screen. The reading desk is dated 1671 and the pulpit goes with it. The choir stalls and box pews incorporate 17th and 18th century woodwork. The monuments include slates to John Isaak of Parc, d1733, children of John Jones, d1797-8 and John Edmunds of Parc, d1800.

LLANGELYNIN   *St Celynin*   SH 751737

Access to this remotely located single chamber above the Conwy valley is across fields. It has a 15th century oak doorway on the south side and an unrestored interior with slab floors and rough plasterwork, 17th century trusses over the nave and older arch-braced trusses further east. The square-headed east window with three cusped lights is 16th century but beside it there remains an older niche. The south windows of two lights are 17th century. The north chapel has a late 16th century roof and an ogival-headed east lancet of c1400, perhaps reset. Traces survive of the chancel screen and its former loft, and there are late 17th century altar rails and a reredos. The octagonal font may be 14th century. There is an 18th century two-decker pulpit and the reading desk incorporates Elizabethan panels. A holy well with seats lies south of the church.

Llangelynin Church

Llangelynin Church

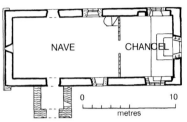

Plan of Llangelynin Church

LLANGELYNIN   *St Celynin*   SH 571072

This single chamber set into the hillside has a west wall with a battered base and one slit window low down perhaps of c1200. There are opposed north and south doorways with low pointed heads with voussoirs. In the 16th century a new two-light window was provided on the south side of the sanctuary and the side walls were heightened to take a fine new roof of shallower pitch. Curved braces from wall-posts support each tie-beam with a kingpost and vertical struts. Only the central strip with rosettes remains of the original celure at the east end. The massive 17th century porch has a bellcote over the outer arch. The east window is 18th century. Most of the furnishings are of 1823 but the screen has late medieval panels, the octagonal font is 13th century and the commandments are given in Welsh on a board of 1797. The figure of Death painted on the north wall is probably late 17th century, and there is an 18th century horse bier on the south side. There is a monument to Mary Thomas of Hendre, d1785.

LLANGIAN   *St Cian*   SH 295289

The western two thirds of the single chamber represent the church mentioned in 1254. The eastern end and the roof of arch-braced collar-trusses represent a late 15th century remodelling. The other features are of 1858, and 1906, when the porch was added. The octagonal font is of 1638, The earliest of the monuments to the Edwards family of Nanhoron is that of Timothy, d1780. There are also hatchments to them. South of the church is a granite pillar with a 5th or 6th century inscription referring to a doctor.

Llangian Church

Llangower Church

Llangelynin Church

LLANGOWER   *St Cywair*   SH 903323

This small building south of Lake Bala has some old walling and square-headed 17th or 18th century windows, the date 1722 appearing over one on the south side. The font pillar and base are 15th century but the circular bowl may be 12th century.

LLANGWNNADL   *St Gwynhoedl*   SH 208333

An inscription on a pier records the addition in 1520 of wide north and south aisles onto a modest single chamber probably of 13th century origin, resulting in a building wider than it is long. There are arcades of three bays with four-centred arches. Only on the south side do the piers have capitals. Original are the roofs of arched-braced collared trusses, the moulded south doorway, the octagonal font with heads and flowers, and the east windows with fragments of old glass, that of the north aisle having a hoodmould with headstops. The side windows are of 1850. In the south aisle east wall is a boulder with a 6th century incised cross. Against this wall is a slate to John Lloyd, d1667. The north aisle has a similar slate to Catherine Owen, d1717.

LLANGWSTENIN   *St Gwstenin*   SH 822792

A monument to Catherine Lloyd, d1799 and fragments of stained glass of c1500 depicting the Resurrection, St Catheine, St George, St Nicholas and St Peter are the only features older than the complete rebuilding of 1843.

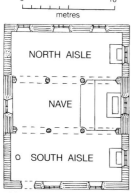

Plan of Llangwnnadl Church

Llangwnnadl Church

Llaniestyn Church

13th Century	15h Century
14th Century	Later

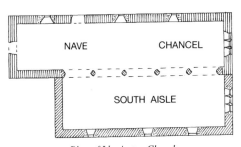

Plan of Llaniestyn Church

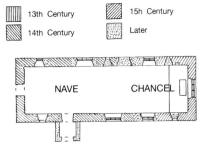

Plan of Llangybi Church

LLANGYBI   *St Cybi*   SH 428412

The church was much restored in 1879 but appears to be a 14th century building extended eastwards in the 15th century. The west doorway and east window plus the octagonal font are medieval. The altar-table is dated 1736 with the initials WP and RT. A stone with a 7th to 9th century Celtic cross stands beside the lychgate.

LLANIESTYN   *St Iestyn*   SH 270337

The south nave and the arcade of five four-centred arches is late 15th century. Projecting beyond it is the 13th century western part of the north nave with a lancet on each side (the southern one blocked) and a pair of late lancets over a late medieval west doorway. The three lancets of the east end of the north nave may be of c1300. The south nave has a similar but later window. There are monuments to Evanus Saethon, d1639, Reverend Ellis Anwil, d1724 and Reverend Owen Owen, d1765.

LLANLLECHID   *St Llechid*   SH 623687

The church was entirely rebuilt in 1844. The octagonal font may be older and has an 18th century cover.

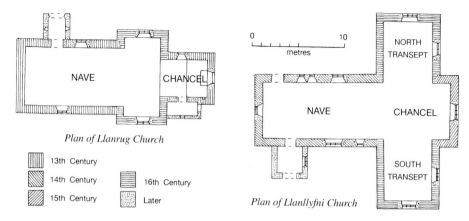

Plan of Llanrug Church

▦ 13th Century

▨ 14th Century

▧ 15th Century

▤ 16th Century

⣿ Later

Plan of Llanllyfni Church

LLANLLYFNI *St Rhedyw* SH 471578

The 14th century nave has a north doorway with voussoirs, large west quoins and a roof of arch-braced trusses on wall-posts. In the 15th century chancel and 16th century transepts the arch-braced trusses are more rounded. The windows are all of the restoration of 1879. The base of the font is also late medieval.

LLANNOR *Holy Cross* SH 354372

The nave and chancel are 13th century but were mostly rebuilt in 1855 when the Bodvel family chapel on the south side was removed. A new south transept further west was added in 1905. The octagonal font and the lower part of the tall west tower are late medieval. The saddleback tower roof is 19th century. In the porch are a 6th century inscribed stone and an early 17th century tablet with a shield of arms and initials of Huw Gwyn and Thomas Bodfel. Over the entrance is a slate with low-relief angels to John Owens, Chancellor of Bangor and vicar here in 1723-37.

LLANRHYCHWYN *St Rhychwyn* SH 775616

The church is remotely located high above the Conwy valley. The south and west walls of the south nave represent Llywelyn Fawr's early 13th century church, but the font may be still earlier. The south nave was extended in the 15th century and has an east window of that period with old stained glass below a date-stone of 1753. The doorway has voussoirs and the door itself is 16th or 17th century and hung on a post hinge in the Roman manner. Several windows are 17th century. The north nave was added by Maredudd ap Madog c1520 and has an arcade of horizontal beams carried on three square piers and some old glass in the east window. This part has a bellcote in which is a 14th century bell and a roof in which the trusses are spaced further apart towards the east end. The north windows have old stained glass of various periods. The altar rails are of 1636, the two-decker pulpit is of 1691 and the reading desk is 18th century.

LLANRUG *St Michael* SH 538637

The shallow transepts may be 16th century, the nave and chancel are probably 13th or 14th century and the bellcote is perhaps of 1767, the date marked on the bell. The wooden north doorway and the roof trusses are probably 16th century. The fourth truss from the west has hammerbeams. All the windows are of the restoration of 1856.

Llanrwst Church

LLANRWST   *St Grwst*   SH 798616

A good rood screen of c1500 with emblems of the Passion and pigs eating acorns on the tracery divides the late medieval main body with an original arch-braced roof, south doorway and windows. Over the screen is a loft with niches on the western parapet. The east window is of four lights with panel tracery and a transom. The font is probably 17th century and there are late 18th century Royal Arms. The west tower, north aisle and south porch are 19th century. In 1633-4 Sir Richard Wynn of Gwydir added a fine south chapel with battlements, pinnacles and windows with cusped lights. It has a screen towards the chancel and contains original panelling and Jacobean style desk fronts. There is a stone coffin with sunk quatrefoils, supposedly that of Llywelyn Fawr, d1240 from the abbey of Aberconwy. There are effigies of Hywel Coetmor, c1440, Sir John Wynn, d1627, and his wife Sydney, and the young Sydney Wynn, d1639, plus a unique series of lozenge-shaped brasses with busts of 17th century members of the Wynn family. One of them, with a complete figure, is signed Sylvanus Crue.

LLANSANTFFRAID GLAN CONWY   *St Ffraid*   SH 803761

Of a double-naved late medieval building the rebuilding of 1839 left only some stained glass figures of c1500 of St John the Baptist and St Catherine in the west window.

LLANUWCHLLYN   *St Deiniol*   SH 874302

The only features older than the rebuilding of 1873 are a monument of c1720 to Ellis Lewis and his family and a fine recumbent effigy of the late 14th century knight Ieuan ap Gruffydd ap Madog ap Iorwerth.

LLANWNDA   *St Gwyndaf*   SH 477587

The church was rebuilt in 1846 but contains monuments to Owen Meridith, d1612, Thomas Bulkeley, d1708, Mrs Lumley Bulkeley, d1718, Lady Elinor Williams, d1719, Anne Quellyn and Hugh Quellyn, d1730 and 1749, and Catherina Quellyn, d1746.

LLANYMAWDDWY   *St Tydecho*   SH 858148

An octagonal 12th century font with scallops was the only ancient feature to survive the rebuilding of the nave and addition of a new chancel in 1854.

MAENTWROG   *St Twrog*   SH 664405

A new church of 1814 replacing the medieval building was itself remodelled in 1896. Inside are monuments to Anne Meyrick of Berthlwyd, d1743 and Robert Gruffydd of Tanybwlch, d1750. Against the SW corner lies the Maen-Twrog, a stone supposedly hurled by St Twrog from the top of Maelwyn to destroy a pagan altar.

MALLWYD   *St Tydecho*   SH 863124

Originally this was a chapel-of-ease to Llanymawddwy. The western part retains a medieval priest's doorway with voussoirs. The biblical scholar Dr John Davies was vicar here from 1604 to 1644. In 1624 he added the more thinly walled chancel with its four-light east window with a transom and ceiling upon close-spaced trusses with big collars. The head of what may have been an older east window dated 1613 lies beside the south wall. In 1640-1 Davies added the timber-framed south porch and the west bell-tower. The windows on the south side carried up through the roof into dormers are 18th century. Some of the tie-beams and struts of the roof were removed to open out the view of a late 18th century gallery backed against the piers carrying the tower. The font and the altar table both were given in 1734 by John Mytton.

NANT PERIS   *St Peris*   SH 607582

This is the mother church of Llanberis, although it lies nowhere near that village. A modest single chamber of the 13th or 14th century with its north doorway still surviving was later given transepts and a new chancel. In the 17th century the eastern re-entrant angles of this extended cruciform building were filled in by family chapels and the whole building re-roofed. The crossing has octagonal piers at the eastern corners. Parts still remain of the screen and loft of c1500 which originally stood in the west arch of the crossing but has been moved further east. There is a tablet to Mary Morgan, d1779.

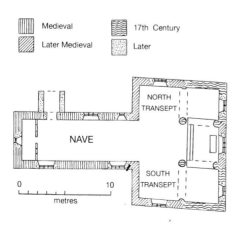

Plan of Nant Peris Church

Mallwyd Church

PENLLECH   *St Mary*   SH 220344

The circular font bowl is probably medieval but the church and its furnishings are otherwise all of the 1840s.

PENMACHNO   *St Tudclud*   SH 790506

The church itself is of 1859-63. The font may be 12th century and there is in the chancel an important collection of stones with interesting 5th and 6th century inscriptions.

PENMORFA   *St Beuno*   SH 548407

The 13th or 14th century nave with the walls battered inside was extended in the late medieval period. The south doorway and fragments of stained glass in a west window are 16th century and the porch and vestry are 18th century, The church was much restored in 1899. There are tablets to William Maurice of Clennau, d1622, and Emmanuel Annwyl, d1646, and a cartouche of 1700 to Sir John Owen, d1666.

PENNAL   *St Peter ad Vincula*   SH 699004

The wide single chamber with square-headed side windows is probably of 1761 with additions of a porch in 1880 and a vestry in 1901. The roof has arched braces with kingposts above. The 18th century furnishings include a goblet type font, supports for a former west gallery, and four oak roundels showing St Andrew, St Jude, St Paul and St Mary Magdalene probably from Belgium or Holland. The many monuments include those of Humphrey Edwards of Talgarth, d1772, and Hugh Vaughan, d1717.

PENRHOS   *St Cynwyl*   SH 346344

There is a monument to Gruffudd ap John Wynn, d1613 in the church of 1842, which replaced an older building with a thatched roof.

PENTIR   *St Cedol*   SH 572671

There is a monument to Hugh Williams, d1754 and his wife, d1782 and family in the church of 1848 which replaced the late 17th century Llangodol chapel further north.

PENTREFELIN   *St Cynhaearn*   SH 525388

The cruciform church of c1832 replaced the former Ystumllyn Chapel to the west.

Pistyll Church

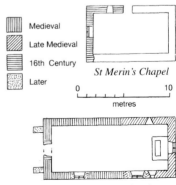

Medieval
Late Medieval
16th Century
Later

St Merin's Chapel

0   10
metres

Plan of Pistyll Church

PISTYLL   *St Beunol*   SH 326420

This small rustic single chamber lies by the pilgrimage route southwards from Clynnog Fawr to Bardsey Island. The font with scallops and overlapping ovals with a horizontal band is 12th century or earlier and an early blocked doorway remains on the south side. The east end is later medieval and has a slit window on each side. The west doorway and shallow-pitched arch-braced roof are 16th century. There are traces of a painting of St Christopher on the north wall.

PWLLHELI   *St Peter*   SH 373353

The church of 1887 replacing one of 1834 contains a seven-sided font probably from the demolished medieval parish church of St Deneio.

RHIW   *St Aelrhiw*   SH 222279

The cruciform church was mostly rebuilt and refurnished in 1860-61.

ST MERINS   *St Merin*   SH 537697

A gable and foundations of a tiny chapel lie hidden in wooded cleft above the sea.

TALYLLYN   *St Mary*   SH 711094

The main feature of interest is the 15th century roof of the main body with arch-braced collar trusses to the west, tie-beam trusses in the middle and a 16th century celure at the east with slender ribs, and painted rosettes and bearded faces for bosses. Panels from a former west gallery are used to close off the 16th century south chapel for modern use as a vestry. The west wall with regular blocks and a bellcote on a wall-pier must be 18th century. The square font is 12th century. The altar table and the rails around it are late 18th century.

The painted celure at Talyllyn Church

Trefriw Church

TRAWSFYNYDD *St Madryn*   SH 708358

The older northern nave extended considerably to the west of the 16th century south nave until rebuilt in a shorter form after a fire in 1978. A row of six octagonal posts of uncertain date divides the naves. The south porch is also 16th century, the doorway having rough voussoirs. The other features are Victorian.

TREFLYS   *St Michael*   SH 534378

The nave may be 13th century. The west doorway has voussoirs and monolithic jambs, New lancets and a chancel arch were provided in a rebuilding of 1888. The medieval font is from St Catherine's Church at Criccieth. In the church is a stone with a Chi-Rho symbol and a 6th century inscription found in the churchyard wall in 1904.

TREFRIW   *St Mary*   SH 781632

The south nave is early 15th century and the north nave is early 16th century. The roofs with arch-braced collar-trusses survived the restoration of c1850. Panels reused in the pulpit are dated 1653 and have shells, leaves, grotesque human heads and cherubs. Other panels of that period are reused in the pews. There are oval plaques to Rector Thomas Jones, d1759 and Jane Hughes of Gomanog, d1778.

■	12th Century	▨	15th Century
▥	13th Century	▦	Later

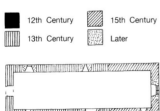

Plan of Treflys Church

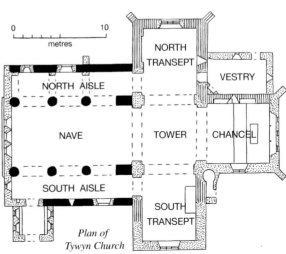

0 — 10
metres

NORTH TRANSEPT

VESTRY

NORTH AISLE

NAVE   TOWER   CHANCEL

SOUTH AISLE

SOUTH TRANSEPT

Plan of Tywyn Church

Font at Tywyn

Tywyn Church

TYWYN   *St Cadfan*   SH 588010

In the early 13th century a central tower with transepts and a chancel were erected east of a 12th century aisled nave with round-headed clerestory windows over round-arched arcades carried on circular piers. The monastery founded by St Cadfan probably still functioned in its original unreformed Celtic format when the nave was built. The original tower collapsed in 1692 and in 1736 a low west tower was inserted into the fourth bay of the nave. The south doorway and the arches across the north aisle may also be of that period. In the restoration of 1881-84 the west tower was removed and a new west wall provided, thus shortening the building by one bay. A new central tower was erected and the chancel and south transept mostly rebuilt. The north transept has an original east lancet and later medieval diagonal buttresses. The chancel north wall has an original lancet over two recesses containing effigies of a 14th century priest and a knight drawing his sword, possibly Gruffydd ap Adda, d1331. Other monuments include those of Vincent Corbett, d1723, Athelstan Owen, 1731, and Ann Dafydd, d1785. The whitewashed nave has a late medieval roof with quatrefoils above massive trusses. The south porch was added c1920. There is a square 13th century font. A pillar stone of c750 with a barely visible Welsh inscription is the earliest known record of the language.

YSBYTY IFAN   *St John the Baptist*   SH 844489

The last remains of a church of the Knights Hospitallers founded c1190 were swept away in a rebuilding of the 1850s, but some notable monuments survive. There is a slab showing a hare below a shield to Cynwrig, son of Llywarch, c1330. There are two other fragmentary 14th century slabs and three damaged 16th century effigies said to be of Rhys Fawr ap Meredydd, his wife Lowry, and their son Robert, who was chaplain to Cardinal Wolsey. A brass shows Robert and Anne Gethin, d1598 with clasped hands, an infant in a shroud and six other children.

GAZETTEER OF CHURCHES OF DENBIGHSHIRE & FLINTSHIRE

ABERGELE   *St Michael*   SH 945777

The west tower, the roofs, the much restored screen and several of the windows including those of five lights at the east end of this unusually long double-naved church are all of c1475-1540. The west doorway of the aisle is of large stones and lacks a chamfer. The westernmost arch of the eight bay arcade dates only from 1858. The tower top stage and buttresses are of 1861 and the porch is of 1887. The foundations on the south side represent either a chantry chapel or a priest's lodging. One north window contains fragments of medieval glass. The font of 1663 stands on an older base. The 17th century pulpit has patterns of fruit, leaves and flowers. There are fragments of several 14th century crosses, a late 14th century floriated cross-slab, a dug-out chest. The best of the several 18th century tablets is that to Catherine Parry, d1706.

BANGOR IS-COED   *St Dunawd*   SJ 388454

No traces remain of the large and important Celtic monastery here. The earliest relics are the 14th century arcades and the chancel with reticulated tracery in the five-light east window. The north arcade was originally one bay longer. The north aisle eastern half was rebuilt in 1832, having previously been wider with three cross-gables. The vestry east of it was added in 1913. Richard Trubshaw's brick and stone west tower of 1726 has pilaster buttresses and urn-like finials. In 1877 the south aisle was rebuilt one bay longer and the north porch added. The late medieval font bears the Instruments of The Passion and emblems of the four Evangelists in shields. The reredos of 1725 now lies at the west end. There is a monument to the Reverend John Fletcher, d1741.

BERSE DRELINCOURT   SJ 316510

This church was built by Mary Drelincourt, widow of a Dean of Armagh, in 1742 to serve a girls' charity school she had founded in 1719. Apart from the ceiling, which is flat at the sides and tunnel-vaulted in the middle, the church has been much altered. It was extended westwards in 1828. Parts of the pulpit and one chandelier are original. A chandelier of 1688 and the altar table have come from the church at Wrexham.

Abergele Church

Aisle west doorway at Abergele

Bangor Is-Coed Church

BETWS GWERFYL GOCH   *St Mary*   SJ 032465

Late medieval are the south doorway formed of just three stones, the arch-braced roof and the panels from a former screen in the reredos. The timber south porch is dated 1606. The pulpit is of 1741.

BODFARI   *St Stephen*   SJ 093701

The west tower has 15th century belfry openings but may be older. Otherwise only the 15th century font, the altar-table and pulpit of 1635, and the chest dated 1675 survived the rebuilding of 1865 when a timber south arcade was removed. See p10.

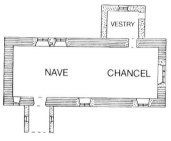

Plan of Betws Gwerfyl Goch Church

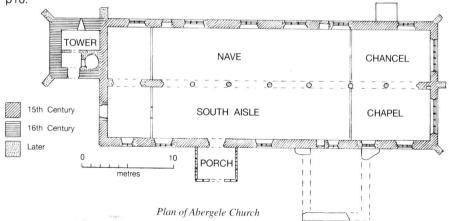

Plan of Abergele Church

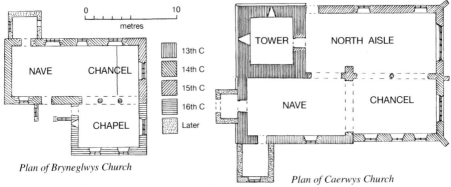

Plan of Bryneglwys Church

Plan of Caerwys Church

BRYNEGLWYS   *St Tysilio*   SJ 145472

The walls and arch-braced roof of the main body may be 14th century. The wagon roof and window at the east end are 15th century. The Yale Chapel with wooden pillars and two windows in the main body are late 16th century. The pulpit is Jacobean and panels of 1615 are incorporated in the stalls of 1875. There are angel-heads on the font. A 14th century slab has an inscription to Tangwystl, daughter of Ieuaf ap Maredudd.

CAERWYS   *St Michael*   SJ 127728

The NW tower and the nave were built immediately after Edward granted the town a charter in 1290. A new chancel with a tomb recess in the south wall was added c1350-70. The wide north aisle extending the whole length of the church east of the tower has a 15th century roof and east window. The wooden arcade was replaced by stone arches in 1894. The font and altar table are dated 1620 and there is old woodwork in the pulpit, screen and panelling. There are several 14th century tomb slabs, part of a female effigy of c1300 possibly the wife of Dafydd ap Gruffydd, and a pair of similar tablets to Thomas Mostyn and the Reverend Thomas Lewis, who both died in 1751.

Caerwys Church

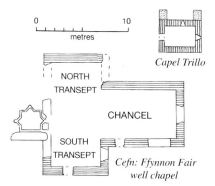

0 _____ 10
metres

Capel Trillo

NORTH TRANSEPT

CHANCEL

SOUTH TRANSEPT

Cefn: Ffynnon Fair well chapel

Old postcard of Capel Trillo

CAPEL TRILLO   *St Trillo*   SH 084812

Beside the coast road is a tiny vaulted chapel just 3.3m long by 2.3m wide inside. The slit windows and pointed west doorway with voussoirs suggest a 13th century date.

CEFN: FFYNNON FAIR   *St Mary*   SJ 068711

The ruined chapel probably built c1500 under patronage of the Stanley family has a chancel with a south doorway and two windows, and shallow transepts, one with a bellcote and the other with a window and doorway. The star-planned holy well lies in the SE corner of a nave that was probably never built.

CERRIG-Y-DRUDION   *St Mary Magdalene*   SH 954486

The single chamber was enlarged in 1503 and the roof may be of that period. The SE chapel and the porch are probably 17th century. An 18th century bracketed bowl forms the font. The west wall and the existing windows except for two narrow slits are of 1874. The chest dates from 1715. There are monuments to Thomas Price, d1658 and Margaret Price, d1723.

CHIRK   *St Mary*   SJ 291377

The main body has a Norman-look-ing clasping buttress at the SE cor-ner and a blocked south doorway. The windows are of the 15th cen-tury when a wide north aisle with a three bay arcade and a diagonally-buttressed tower at its west end were added. The aisle has a roof of arched-braced trusses carved with animals, and pseudo-hammer beams. There are chests of 1675 and 1736, a font of 1662, and there are 17th century carved panels in the pulpit and reading desk.

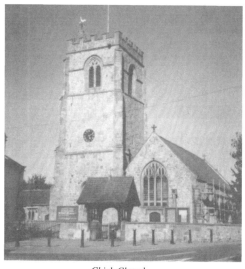

Chirk Church

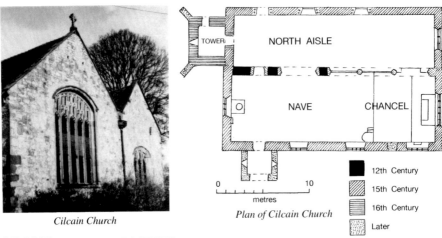

Cilcain Church

Plan of Cilcain Church

TOWER
NORTH AISLE
NAVE
CHANCEL

0
10
metres

■ 12th Century
▨ 15th Century
▤ 16th Century
▦ Later

CILCAIN   *St Mary*   SJ 177652

Some 12th century walling remains in the nave north wall. In it is an arch dating from the 15th century when the original north aisle, of which a three bay arcade remains further east, was widened and extended westwards by two bays. The splendid nave roof of c1500 with alternate arched-braced and hammer-beam trusses and a wagon ceiling at the east end may be imported from elsewhere. There are angels with emblems of The Passion on the hammer beams. The north windows and doorway are of 1764, and the upper stage and buttresses of the late medieval tower are of 1888. There are fragments of several 14th century coffin lids with crosses and effigies, and a font with interlacing, There is a monument of 1731 to several members of the Mostyn family.

CLOCAENOG   *St Meddwid*   SJ 084542

The walls of the single chamber may be 14th century. The font is perhaps 15th century and of the 1530s are the east window, the north doorway, the arch-braced roof, and the screen. Panels from the rood loft have been re-used in the altar rails. There is a dug-out chest. The pulpit is of 1695 and the wooden chandelier is of 1725. There is a monument of c1705 to Evan Lloyd ap Rice and several other relatives.

CORWEN   *St Mael & St Sulien*   SJ 079434

This 13th century church was once cruciform although there is now no south transept and a narrow aisle of 1871 with a four-bay arcade now extends along that side. West of the new aisle is a vestry of 1898, and also Victorian are the north porch, the north transept end wall, and the battlements on the west tower. Original features are the small triple east lancets of the chancel and the single lancets on each side of the north transept. The nave has a medieval roof with large tiebeams, collars and crown-posts (one truss is dated 1687) and the north transept has a 15th century roof with arch-braced collar-trusses. In the chancel is an effigy of the 14th century priest Iorwerth Suliem. Other monuments include those of Maria Charlotte Lloyd of Rhug, 1780, Roger Jones of Cefn Rug, d1790, John Jones of Rhagatt, d1797 and Margaret Parry, d1800. The cable-moulded font is 12th century. There is an ancient dug-out chest. The church was served by five priests in 1291, having long been a Celtic monastic site. A 9th or 10th century sandstone cross-shaft stands outside by the tower.

Corwen Church

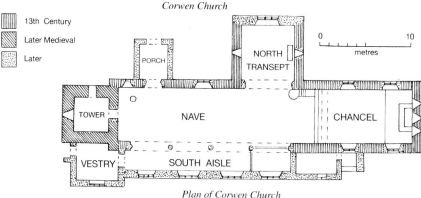

Plan of Corwen Church

CWM   *St Mael & Sulien*   SJ 075776

The steps in the floor of the single chamber reflect the sloping nature of the site of this church. A tomb recess has re-used 14th century work but the doorways and the south and east windows suggest a rebuilding c1480-1520. The porch and the north windows may be 17th century and one south window is of 1769. There are three 14th century tomb-slabs with crosses, a fragment of the head of a standing cross, and a hooded tombstone to Grace Williams, d1642 which lies outside the church.

CYFFYLLIOG   *St Mary*   SJ 059577

The 14th century single chamber lies by the River Clywedog. The east window has intersecting tracery. One north window and the wagon roof at the east end are 15th century. The south doorway and porch were removed in 1876, and a west porch was added in 1903-4. The font has been recut. There is a dug-out chest, and a more recent chest dates from 1687. Parts of the old screen have been reused in the stalls, pulpit and communion rails.

Ruins of Leicester's Church at Denbigh

Tower of St Hilary's, Denbigh

DENBIGH   *St Hilary*   SJ 053657

Only the west tower now survives of a large nave and chancel church of c1300 within the late 13th century town walls. The church had a crypt below the chancel and was given a wide north aisle in the 18th century. It was demolished in 1904, a more conveniently sited new church of St Mary having been built at the bottom of the hill in 1874.

Also within the town walls lies the shell of a large aisled rectangular church begun by Robert Dudley, Earl of Leicester in 1578, probably with the intention of making it a cathedral in place of that at St Asaph. It was abandoned still unfinished in 1584. It had round-arched arcades on alternate double and single Tuscan columns and large windows with flat four-centred heads with uncusped tracery.

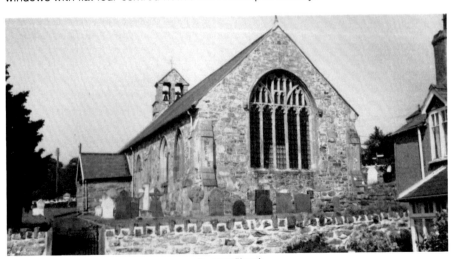

Derwen Church

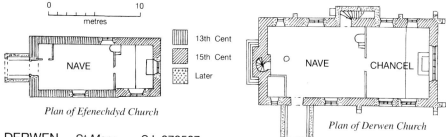

▥	13th Cent
▨	15th Cent
▦	Later

Plan of Efenechdyd Church

Plan of Derwen Church

DERWEN   *St Mary*   SJ 070507

The single chamber has a staircase in a projection on the north side leading to a rood-loft over a fine screen of c1500. Also of that period are the arch-braced roof, the five-light east window, and a more modest north window, but some of the walling may be older. The font is dated 1665 and the double bellcote was formerly dated 1688. In the churchyard is a fine 15th century cross with niches in the head containing scenes of the Coronation of the Virgin, the Crucifixion, the Virgin and Child, and an angel, perhaps St Michael, with scales.

DYSERTH   *St Bridget & St Cwyfan*   SJ 055793

The nave has a 13th century south doorway and massive later medieval west buttresses. The narrower chancel inclines to the north and has a fine east window with stained glass of 1450 and c1540, the latter being a Jesse Tree. The north transept and vestry were added in 1873-5. In the nave are tomb-slabs of c1330 and c1400 with crosses, plus fragments of a 12th century churchyard cross with spirals, double heads and plaits.

EFENECHDYD   *St Michael*   SJ 112556

The 14th century chancel with a renewed east window and the older nave form a single chamber to which a west porch has been added. The roof is medieval and there is a rare wooden font bowl with fourteen facets with beads at the bottom. There is some 17th century panelling in the pulpit and parts of the low screen are late medieval.

Dyserth Church

Gresford Church

GRESFORD   *All Saints*   SJ 346549

This splendid all-embattled church with arcades of seven bays for aisles with two bay chapels screened off at their east ends appears from a cursory glance to be all of c1480-1530. However the NW buttress of the 13th century nave survives, and of the early 14th century are the south aisle west window, the lower part of the diagonally-buttressed west tower with a staircase in the SW corner, and the crypt below the chancel east end. The main arcade piers have eight shafts with deep hollows between them. The chapels have towards the chancel a full arch on the west and doorways on the east. The latter formed part of a processional way around the high altar until the arrangement was changed in the 1630s to comply with Archbishop Laud's reforms. Work on the spectacular upper stages of the tower dragged on from the 1520s until the 1580s. The south porch is also 16th century. See picture on page 13.

There are a very fine set of medieval screens. The choir stalls have misericords carved with various creatures plus scenes of the Devil wheeling souls to hell and the Annunciation. There are chandeliers of 1747 and 1796 and benefaction boards of 1731. The splendid set of stained glass windows, mostly sponsored by the Stanley Earl of Derby c1500 were much restored in the 19th century and again most recently after unfortunately treated with detergent by a church cleaning company in 1966. They include a Jesse Tree and Te Deum in the east window and numerous figures of saints and biblical scenes.

The many monuments include damaged 14th century effigies of a bishop and a civilian, the knight Madog ap Llywelyn ap Gruffydd, d1331, the legs and bust of John Trevor, d1589, a kneeling figure of Dame Katherine Trevor, d1602 with her daughters, kneeling figures of the 1630s of the same Dame Katherine with her husband Sir Richard Trevor, a tablet of 1659 to Anthony Lewis, a cartouche to John Robinson, c1680, and tablets to John Travers, d1748, and his wife.

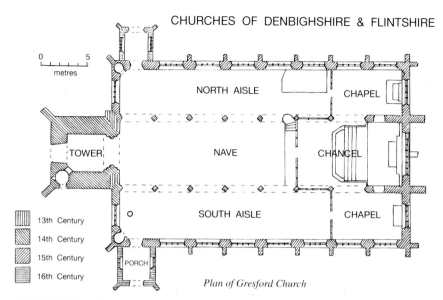

0 _____ 5
metres

NORTH AISLE

CHAPEL

TOWER

NAVE

CHANCEL

13th Century

14th Century

15th Century

16th Century

SOUTH AISLE

CHAPEL

PORCH

Plan of Gresford Church

GWAUNYSGOR   *St Mary Magdalene*   SJ 074811

The north doorway suggests that the western part of the single chamber may be 13th century, like the font set upon five shafts. The eastern part is 15th century. The barrel-vaulted porch is 16th century and the south doorway, freestanding on two posts in a wider arch, may be 17th century. The altar table is dated 1637. There are various fragments of 13th and 14th century tomb slabs bearing crosses, swords and circles.

GWYDDELWERN   *St Beuno*   SJ 075467

The chancel has been rebuilt above plinth level but retains a blocked doorway in the south side in an unusual position hard up against the chancel arch. There are also two reset 14th century windows with Y-tracery and some early 16th century parts in the roof. The nave has three 15th century windows on the south side, where there is a Victorian porch-tower, and two more on the north side. Also 15th century are the font and parts of the dado of the screen. The reredos has 17th century panels with relief scenes of birds and dragons. Another panel is dated 1705. Stained glass of c1500 with two saints' heads remains in the chancel windows. There is a monument to William Humphreys, d1718 and his wife, d1744.

GWYTHERIN

St Winefred   SH 877617

In the single chamber rebuilt in 1867-9 are an old font, a dug-out chest and two floriated cross-slabs. One has a chalice and commemorates the priest Llayerch Capellanus.

Gwaunysgor Church

Hanmer Church

HALKYN   *St Mary*   SJ 209712

The church was entirely rebuilt in 1877-8. Reset on a south buttress is a 14th century Crucifixion with St Mary and St John from the head of a former churchyard cross.

HANMER   *St Chad*   SJ 456398

The tall west tower with springers for an intended rib-vault, and the embattled aisles with windows of four and five lights are essentially all of c1450-1500. The short chancel was built in 1720. The nave and aisles were re-roofed and given new four-bay arcades and a south porch after a fire in 1889, although the chancel was not restored until 1936. The chandelier of 1727 is from Bangor cathedral. Other old furnishings and monuments all perished in the fire.

HAWARDEN   *St Deiniol*   SJ 315659

Parts of the chancel are 13th century with restored sedilia. The nave arcades of three bays and the chancel arch are 14th century and the central tower inserted into the nave east bay is 15th century. Most of the aisle outer walls are 14th century work, and there is a reset piscina of that period in the north aisle, but the doorways and windows and the piers supporting the arcades, plus the spire on the tower are all of the 1850s. The large south chapel has 14th or 15th century walling but lacks any ancient features. On the north side is a chapel built to contain the tomb of William Gladstone completed in 1906. There is a monument Roger Whitney, d1722. On the reverse of a brass inscription to John Price, d1684, are shown a canopy and the upper parts of figures of a man and woman of c1630.

Tower at Henllan Church

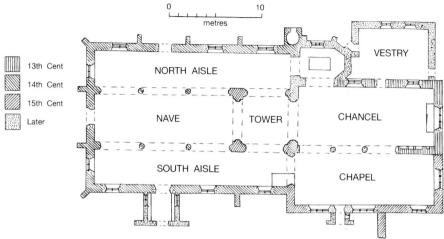

Plan of Hawarden Church

HENLLAN   *St Sadwn*   SJ 022682

The large single chamber has a 14th century piscina and north doorway and a renewed 15th century east window. The other features are of 1805-8 and 1878-9, but there is a Jacobean altar table with melon bulb legs. Commanding the church from a rock to the SE is a detached tower of uncertain date with paired lancets for bell openings.

Hawarden Church

The well chapel at Holywell

Holt Church

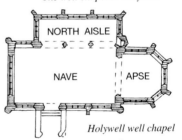

Holywell well chapel

HOLT   *St Chad*   SJ 413541

The five-bay arcades with sharply pointed arches and the reset piscina in the chancel are probably of c1290-1310 when the Warenne family built the castle and laid out the village. The west tower is later 14th century, although it bears the date 1679 referring to repairs. It contains a west window of the 1480s when the church was otherwise entirely rebuilt by Sir William Stanley. The south doorway bears the arms of Henry VII in a spandrel, and a bishop and other figures in the jambs, whilst the font of c1493 has heraldry referring to the lords of Bromfield over two centuries. The chancel is flanked by chapels with two bays of four-centred arches on concave-sided octagonal piers. Most of the roof of that period was renewed in 1871. There is a plank chest. A small copper plate to Thomas Crue (Crew), d1666 is by his kinsman Silvanus Crue.

HOLYWELL   *St James*   SJ 186764

The 15th century west tower is embraced by the nave of 1769 with two storey elevations and galleries. A polygonal apse was added in 1884-5. There is a chest of 1679. The monunents include a damaged 13th century effigy of a priest, a cartouche to Robert Edwards, d1694, a monument of c1750 to Edward and Mary Pennant, and several 17th century heraldic tablets.

Font at Holt Church

Well chapel and parish church at Holywell

HOLYWELL   *St Winefride*   SJ 185764

The remarkable chapel just below the west end of the parish church is thought to have been built for Margaret, Countess of Richmond and Derby c1500-10. It has a three bay north aisle and a chancel with a polygonal apse. It was restored in 1976 and lies empty without furnishings. Below the nave and aisle is a fan-vaulted ambulatory set around a star-shaped holy well with a porch to the west, To the north is a large bath for immersion in the mineral waters. St Winefride is said to have been martyred and immediately restored to life on this spot in the 7th century, and it is still an important place for healing and pilgrimage.

HOPE   *St Cynfarch*   ST 495414

The 13th century south aisle with a double piscina, blocked doorway and a crypt below the east end once formed the whole church. The existing nave and chancel north of it with original glass in the east window are of c1500, whilst the diagonally-buttressed tower west of this part may be as late as c1540. The pulpit is Jacobean and there are kneeling effigies of Sir John Trevor of Plas Teg, d1629, and his wife.

ISCOED   *St Mary*   SJ 495414

A former timber-framed chapel-of-ease to Malpas in Cheshire at Whitwell was demolished and replaced in 1830. Amongst the monuments is a tablet from Whitchurch to Philip Henry, d1696.

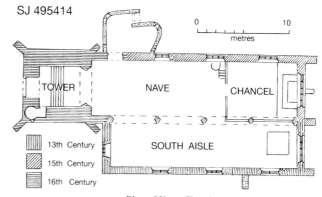

Plan of Hope Church

LLANARMON MYNYDD MAWR   *St Garmon*   S

The small single chamber was mostly rebuilt in 1886. A font bowl of 1717 is built into the vestry wall and the font cover is dated 1723. The altar rails are 18th century.

LLANARMON-YN-IAL   *St Garmon*   SJ 191561

Only the walls, roofs, and the rare brass chandelier with a figure of the Virgin are medieval, the main body being 15th century and the south aisle 16th century. Of the 1730s are the windows, the wooden arcade, and the font and royal arms. There are 14th century effigies of a priest and the knight Gruffydd ap Llywellyn ap Ynyr of Bodidris probably from Valle Crucis Abbey (see page 14), and a mural effigy of Efan Llwyd, c1639.

LLANASA   *St Asaph & St Kentigern*   SJ 106814

The large east windows, the south nave roof and the font of this double-naved church are all 15th century. One north window is of c1600. The north nave roof and arcade were rebuilt in 1739. The other windows and the porch are of 1874. A large west buttress carries a small bell-turret. There is some early 16th century glass. The pulpit is 17th century. There are 14th century tomb slabs. Outside, by the SE corner, is the tomb of Sir Peter Mostyn, d1605.

LLANBEDR DYFFRYN CLWYD   *St Peter*   SJ 145598

The old church near the approach to Llanbedr Hall was abandoned after the new church was built in 1863. The old church had a sandstone 13th century nave and a limestone 15th century east end. The timber-framed porch and one lancet plus several larger later windows have now all disappeared.

LLANDEGLA

St Tegla   SJ 195524

In the church of 1886 is a late medieval brass chandelier with a figure of St Mary.

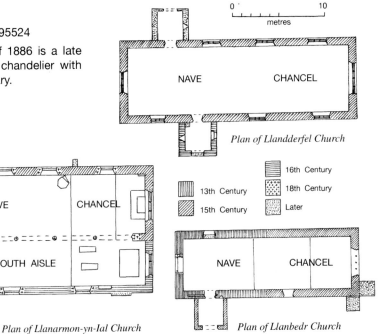

Plan of Llandderfel Church

13th Century

15th Century

16th Century

18th Century

Later

Plan of Llanarmon-yn-Ial Church

Plan of Llanbedr Church

LLANDDERFEL   *St Derfel*   SH 981370

In the late medieval period St Derfel, about whom nothing is now known, was suffi-
ciently venerated to warrant rebuilding the church on a larger scale than would otherwise have been required by a poor mountainous parish. The roof, screen and several
windows are original. The south porch, now a vestry containing a monument to John
Lloyd of Pale, d1742, is 17th century, and the north porch is Victorian. The famous image of St Derfel perched on a stag was burned in London in 1538 along with Friar John
Forest except for the stag (carved from a log and with a defaced head) which still lies
in the church. A stained glass window of the saint is known only from an old sketch.

LLANDRILLO   *St Trillo*   SJ 034371

Only the tower survived a rebuilding of 1876, when it was given an octagonal bell-stage
with a recessed spire. A 14th century font is now disused. A few 18th century memorials to the Lloyds of Hendwr are reset in the organ-chamber. Outside is a an unusually
late example of a hooded tomb chest to Katherine Wynne of Branas, d1706.

LLANDRILLO-YN-RHOS   *St Trillo*   SH 833806

Two 13th century arches, now blocked, have been cut through the north wall of a 12th
or 13th century nave, so there must have once been a north aisle or chapel. The chancel and the south aisle with a four-bay arcade are of c1500 and the tower seems to be
as late as the 1550s. It was once whitewashed to serve as a land-mark for seafarers
and was given a higher SW beacon turret in 1600. The 13th century font has nailhead
decoration. In the porch is a floriated cross-slab to Ednyfed, a 14th century vicar.

Llandrillo-yn-Rhos Church

LLANDYRNOG   *St Teynog*   SJ 108651

The north nave has a roll-moulded 13th century west doorway and both naves have 15th century windows, one of which contains original stained glass. The five bay arcade, belfry, porch and furnishings, except for a dug-out chest, are of 1876-8. There are parts of a 13th century effigy of a priest, and a number of 18th century tablets.

LLANDYSILIO   *St Tysilio*   SJ 195435

This lonely single chamber with an east window, font and arch-braced roofs all of c1500 was given a north chapel in 1718 which was rebuilt in 1869. One north window contains two original stained glass figures. The eagle lectern is medieval. There is a monument to Elizabeth Jones, d1721.

LLANEFYDD   *St Nefydd & St Mary*   SH 982707

This is a little-altered double-naved church with fine roofs and various early 16th century windows and doorways. A west vestry has gone, and the bellcote is Victorian. Against the north wall is the tester of an 18th century pulpit. There are several 14th century tomb slabs, plus a small effigy of Edward ab Iorwerth, and some later tablets.

LLANEILIAN-YN-RHOS   *St Elian*   SH 864765

The slightly wider western part of the north nave may be 12th or 13th century although its blocked doorways are 16th century. The east end, the southern nave and the arch-braced roofs with wagon-ceilings over the altars (the southern one with traces of painted saints) are 15th century. There are fonts of the 17th century and earlier. By the north wall are painted panels from a rood-loft parapet showing the Last Judgement and the legend of St Hubert.

Llaneilian-yn-Rhos Church

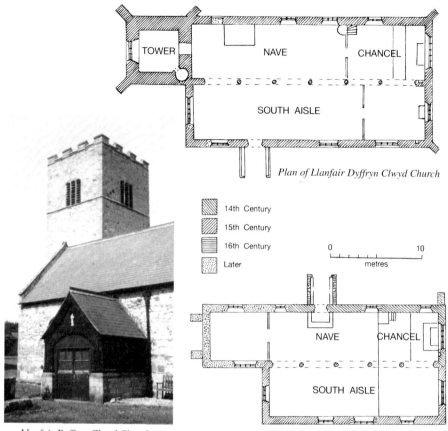

Plan of Llanfair Dyffryn Clwyd Church

14th Century
15th Century
16th Century
Later

0   10
metres

Llanfair Dyffryn Clwyd Church

Plan of Llanelidan Church

LLANELIDAN   *St Elidan*   SJ 110505

The north nave has a 14th century doorway, piscina and window. A Victorian addition extends it westwards beyond the five bay arcade, The late medieval south nave has several original windows and a blocked west doorway. One north window is dated 1618 and the middle southern window bears the year 1626. There are arched-braced roofs with wagon ceilings at the east end. The roll-moulded font may be 15th century. There is some original medieval glass. The pulpit and reredos contain Jacobean wood-work and the altar rails are late 17th century, as are several minor memorial tablets.

LLANFAIR DYFFRYN CLWYD   *St Cynfarch & St Mary*   SJ 135555

The features of the two naves divided by a six-bay arcade are mostly of c1480-1530, and the diagonally buttressed tower beyond the north nave was added in the 1530s. A 14th century cross-slab is set into the blocked north doorway. Stained glass of 1503 remains in one window. There is a large old chest. An early 14th century stone com-memorates Dafydd ap Madog. The font of 1663 and the Jacobean pulpit have gone to the Jesus Chapel of 1787 (founded in 1619) 2km to the SE.

Llanfair Talhaiarn Church

LLANFAIR TALHAIARN   *St Mary*   SH 927702

An offset in the south wall marks the division between the original nave and the later chancel. The arch-braced roofs are partly old and the west doorway is dated 1715, but the six-bay arcade and the windows are mostly of 1876. There are tablets to the Wynnes of Garthewin, notably John, d1692, another John, d1720, and Robert, d1707.

LLANFERRES   *St Berres*   SJ 189606

A font of 1686 with quatrefoils, a dug-out chest, a datestone of 1650, the 16th century east window, several medieval grave-slabs, a 14th century figure of a man standing on a lion, and several 17th and 18th century monuments survived the rebuildings of the church in 1774 and 1843.

LLANFIHANGEL GLYN MYFYR   *St Michael*   SH 991491

The 13th century nave has a doorway dated 1689 with the name of Rector David Wynnew. The west end is of 1853. The wider chancel and the arch-braced roofs are of c1500. There is an old chest. Balusters from an altar rail are reused in the gallery.

LLANFOR   *St Deniol*   SH 938367

Only the much-altered west tower dated 1599 and parts of the 16th century screen survived the total rebuilding of the church in 1874-5.

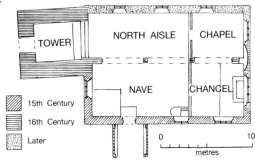

Plan of Llanfwrog Church

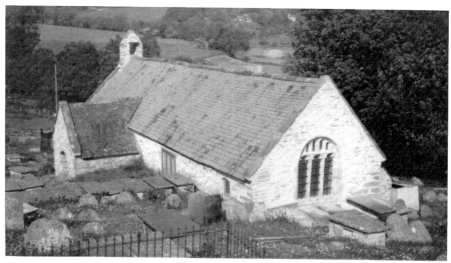

Llangar Church

LLANFWROG   *St Mwrog*   SJ 114578

The south nave has one 15th century window and the porch is partly original. The north nave was mostly rebuilt in 1870 but the three bay arcade with piers of four clustered shafts and the tower west of the nave are mid 16th century.

LLANFYNYDD   *Christ Church*   SJ 280564

In the church of 1842 is a font of c1490 from Hope with the Stanley's eagle's claw badge.

LLANGADWALADR   *St Cadwaladr*   SJ 182304

This remote single chamber was restored in 1840 and given a polygonal apse and new windows in 1883. The roof is partly old. The vestry has a reset 15th century lancet.

LLANGAR   *Dedication Unknown*   SJ 064425

This narrow single chamber has been little used since a new church was built at Cynwyd in 1855 and to it were transferred the monuments to Dorothy Maesmore, d1710, and Edward Lloyd of Plymog, d1742. The arch-braced roof with a coved section above the altar is original. The east window with crude cusping of the lights and the plain mullioned side windows are mid to late 16th century. The porch is dated 1702 and there is a three-decker pulpit. There are wall-paintings of various dates on the north wall.

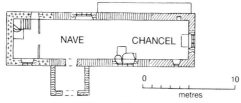

Plan of Llangar Church

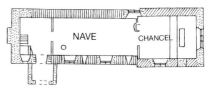

Plan of Llanfihangel Glyn Myfyr Church

Old print of Llangollen Church before restoration

LLANGEDWYN *St Cedwyn* SJ 188242

The church was rebuilt in 1869, leaving only an old font, the 17th century pulpit and chest, woodwork of 1527 reused in the chancel cornice, and monuments of a 14th century priest, Edward and Mary Vaughan, d1718 and 1722, and John Wynne, d1722.

LLANGERYW *St Digain* SH 875674

The south doorway suggests a 13th century date for the nave. The chancel flanked by shallow transepts and the roofs are early 16th century. The windows are of 1849 and 1881. The 15th century font has quatrefoils in circles in squares. There are 17th century altar rails. There are a pair of early pillar stones with crosses incised upon them.

LLANGOLLEN *St Collen* SJ 217419

The church is hemmed in by the town buildings. Until rebuilt and given a south aisle in 1864 it comprised a 13th century nave of which the fine shafted south doorway remains, a 15th century north aisle with a reset 14th century tomb recess, and an 18th century west tower with urns on the corners and round-headed belfry openings above a stage with small circular openings. There are splendid late medieval roofs with hammer beams, bosses and angels, and a brass to Margaret Trevor, d1663.

LLANGWM *St Jerome* SH 966446

The single chamber was mostly rebuilt and given a chancel arch in 1747, and restored and refurnished in 1873. Part of a 14th century heraldic slab is set over the north porch doorway. There is a monument with cherub heads, etc, to Robert Wynne, d1757.

LLANGWYFAN *St Cwyfan* SJ 121663

This little-restored single chamber has a baluster font and box pews. The west and south doorways may be 13th and 14th century respectively. The east end is 15th century with windows of that period on either side. Other side windows and the east window are 17th century, one being dated 1684, whilst the south porch is dated 1714.

Llanrhaeadr-ym-Mochnant Church

LLANGYNHAFAL   *St Cynhafal*   SJ 134633

This double-naved church with a five bay arcade has fine roofs with angels on the hammer beams, a south doorway with a priest carved in the moulding, and several early 16th century windows. The north window is later. The pulpit of 1635 has panels of a lion, a cockatrice and pelican. The altar rails are Georgian. This is an old chest.

LLANHYCHAN   *St Hychen*   SJ 114622

The single chamber has a 15th century west doorway and an arch-braced roof. A window is dated 1626. The reading desk, altar rails, and several tablets are 18th century.

LLANRHAEADR-YM-MOCHNANT   *St Gogfan*   SJ 123260

In the 14th century a new chancel with side chapels was added to the original nave. The chapels have two arches to the chancel and one towards the nave. The wagon ceiling over the high altar is 15th century. It is uncertain when the west tower was begun, but the upper stage with obelisk pinnacles is 18th century. The font is dated 1663 and the altar table is of 1749. There is a rustic monument to Sydney Bynner, d1694. There are fragments of a shrine of c1160 and of an earlier cross-shaft with an angular fret and a grave-slab bearing a wheel-cross.

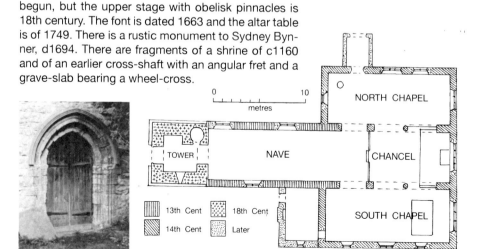

Doorway at Llanynys

Plan of Llanrhaeadr-ym-Mochnant Church

Llanrhudd Church

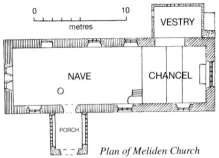

Plan of Meliden Church

LLANRHAEADR-YNG-NGHINMEIRCH   *St Dyfnog*   SJ 082634

The tower west of the south nave may be 14th century. Both naves have fine old roofs and there is a wagon ceiling over the altar in the southern part. The northern of the two good early 16th century east windows contains a stained glass Jesse Tree dated 1533. Other old glass fragments dated 1508, were rescued from a nearby farmhouse in 1830 and reinstated in the west window. A pillar poor box is attached to the dug-out chest. There is a large Baroque monument with a reclining effigy of Maurice Jones, d1702.

LLANRHUDD   *St Meugan*   SJ 140577

This single chamber with an arch-braced roof lies alone 1.5km east of Ruthin, of which it was the original mother church. Two south windows are of c1500, another is later 16th century, and one on the north, now renewed, is dated 1626. The west gallery is dated 1721 and the altar table is 17th century. There are many monuments to the Thel-walls of Bathafan, notably the kneeling effigies of John and Jane, d1586 and 1585, the bust of Ambrose, d1653, and the tablets to John, d1664, and another John, d1686. There is a cartouche to Thomas Roberts, d1708.

LLANSANNAN   *St Sannan*   SH 933657

Medieval walling remains but the two naves were rebuilt in 1777. The windows and the seven bay arcade with timber posts are of 1879. The pulpit was once a three-decker.

LLANSANTFFRAID GLYN DYFRDWY   *St Bride*   SJ 149428

The north and south doorways with plank doors date from 1610, when the church was moved to new site higher above the River Dee. The font may be 12th century. There is a monument to Elizabeth Roberts, d1798. The church was much restored in 1867.

LLANSILIN   *St Silin*   SJ 209282

The 13th century church was cruciform with an aisled nave. Of it there remain the west wall of the nave and the south transept SW corner plus a doorway reset in the outer wall of a south nave probably built to remedy damage sustained during Owain Glyndwr's campaigns. The new nave partly replaced a 14th century chapel west of the transept. The arched-braced south roof with a wagon ceiling at the east end was re-exposed to view in 1890. The tower was added in 1852. The font and cover are probably 17th century and there is an altar table of the 1630s. There are commandment boards in the gallery, a benefaction board of 1740, a dug-out chest, a pillar poor box of 1664, and monuments to Sir William Williams, d1700, David Maurice, d1719, and the Foulkes family, dated 1761 to 1771.

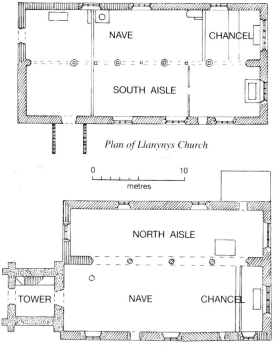

Plan of Llanynys Church

0 ⟶ 10
metres

Plan of Llansilin Church

Llansilin Church

LLANYNYS   *St Saeran*   SJ 103627

The western part of the north nave is 13th century. It contains a damaged 14th century effigy of a priest reset on a tomb chest incorporating 16th and 17th century fragments. The rest of the church is of c1500 except for the porch dated 1544, and the fluted square Doric posts which replaced the arcade c1768. The font is 15th century. There are two 17th century altar tables and much other old woodwork. A wall painting of St Christopher of c1430 was exposed on the north wall in 1967. There is a rare 14th century sepulchral stone which depicts the Crucifixion and a bishop. See page 93.

LLYSFAEN   *St Cynfran*   SH 894767

The north nave is the older part and has a narrow east end built before the south nave was added on. The four-bay arcade was retooled during a heavy restoration by G.E.Street in 1870.

MARCHWEIL   *St Marcellus*   SJ 358477

The nave was rebuilt in 1778 and given a west tower in 1789. A north transept was added in 1829. There is a monument to John Meller, d1736.

MELIDEN   *St Melyd*   SJ 063810

The north doorway is 13th century and the west lancets of 1887 may reproduce originals. The eastern part of the single chamber is probably 15th century although the windows look later. The 13th century font has eight panels with pointed arches.

Mold Church

MOLD   *St Mary*   SJ 242641

Rebuilding began in the 1500s for Margaret Stanley, Countess of Derby and Richmond, and continued under the patronage of Robert Wharton and William Hughes, bishops of St Asaph in 1536-54 and 1573-1600. The nave and aisles have fine arcades with carvings in the spandrels and on the capitals. The rib-vaulted 17th century porch was refaced externally in 1911. The west tower is 18th century but looks almost medieval, and the apsed east bay of the chancel is of 1853. There are fragments of heraldic glass of the 1570s, a brass with a mutilated effigy of Robert Davies, d1602, and several 18th century cartouches.

NANNERCH   *St Mary*   SJ 167698

The church of 1852 contains a fine monument to Charlotte Mostyn, d1694, see p15.

NANTGLYN   *St James*   SJ 004621

Parts of the walling and the arched-braced roof-trusses are medieval. The rest is all of 1862 except for an ancient west doorway seen by Glynne in 1870 but now hidden by slate hanging.

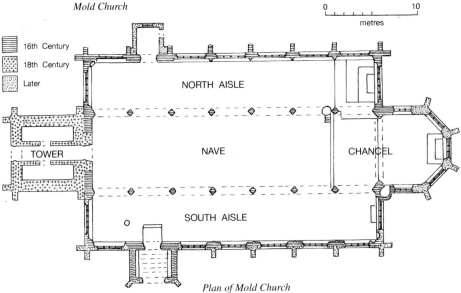

0 — 10 metres

16th Century
18th Century
Later

TOWER   NORTH AISLE   NAVE   CHANCEL   SOUTH AISLE

Plan of Mold Church

NERCWYS   *St Mary*   SJ 235604

The west tower was repaired in 1723. Its arch could be 12th century. The nave has one renewed 14th century window and a later medieval roof with arched braces and cusped wind-braces. Transepts were added in 1847, and a chancel and a cross-gabled north aisle in 1882-4. There is a rare late medieval pulpit and sedilia have been created from fragments of the screen. Richard III's badge of a boar appears on fragments of old glass in the east window. There are fragments of several foliated cross-slabs of c1250-1300, part of a slab with an inscription to Athunyd ferch Dafydd, c1300, two 14th century slabs, a monument to Robert Roberts, d1705, and a chandelier of 1761.

NORTHOP (LLANEURGAIN)   *St Eugain & St Peter*   SJ 246685

The tower was once dated 1571, perhaps the year of completion. In 1839 the church was shortened and the arcade between the original north chamber and the later south aisle was reduced from seven bays to five. Beyond the last arch is a reset 14th century recess. There are four 14th century effigies. The smallest is of Ithel Bleddyn, and the female effigy may be of his wife.

OVERTON   *St Mary*   SJ 374418

The 14th century west tower has diagonal buttresses and a NE staircase turret. The arcades of four normal bays with a narrow extra bay at the west end and also one north window are 15th century. The latter lighted a transept and the rest of the north aisle only attained the same width as this bay in 1819. The south aisle was rebuilt in 1855, and the chancel of 1710 was remodelled in 1870. The parclose screens contain re-used medieval parts from the chancel screen. There is a dug-out chest. Of the 18th century are the baluster font and many tablets. There are numerous old grave-slabs, one of c1300 being to Angharad ferch Einion.

Overton Church

Northop Church

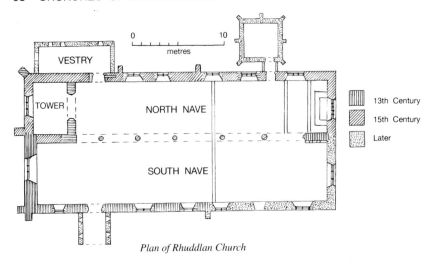

Plan of Rhuddlan Church

RHUDDLAN   *St Mary*   SJ 022781

The long south nave was built c1290 to serve the newly founded Edwardian borough and a chancel was added soon afterwards but has been entirely rebuilt. The north nave was added in the 15th century and a tower was later built within its western bay. Windows of c1480-1520 survive on either side of a mausoleum of 1820 on the north side, but the triple western lancets and other windows were renewed in 1868. A chest is dated 1710 but looks older. There are floriated cross-slabs of c1250-80 and the 14th century. From the nearby Dominican friary church have come parts of effigies of two 14th century friars and an incised slab of William de Freney, Archbishop of Edessa, d1290. He served as a suffragan bishop in England and Wales in his later years.

Rhuddlan Church

RUABON   *St Mary*   SJ 303438

The aisle walls and the west windows are 15th century and the west tower and blocked south doorway are 14th century. The north chapel is a relic of a remodelling of the church in 1770, and the south chapel was added in 1755 to house a tomb of Sir Watkin Williams Wynn of Wynstay. The other windows and the arcades were renewed in 1870-72. The Works of Mercy wall-painting is of the time of the poet-vicar Maredudd ap Rhys, c1430, who wrote about that subject. A 14th century effigy lies in the south aisle, and in the north chapel are effigies on a tomb chest of Sir John ab Ellis Eyton, d1526, and his wife, and standing figures of Henry Wynn, d1719, and his son and daughter-in-law.

RUG   *Holy Trinity*   SJ 064446

This small private manorial chapel on the edge of a park was built in 1637 by Colonel William Salisbury of Rug. The fine original interior was restored during the 1980s. Fittings such as the west gallery, canopied pews, altar rails, benches, panelling and the credence table dated 1632 are all of the period of the chapel, although some may have been imported from other churches in the area. See picture on page 12.

RUTHIN   *St Peter*   SJ 124584

After Reginald de Grey took over the newly begun castle in 1282 he provided a chapel-of-ease here to Llanrhudd. In 1310 John de Grey had the new chapel upgraded into a collegiate church, which was later served by Augustinian Bonhommes. The choir was demolished in 1663, leaving the church as a nave of c1310-20 with a former central tower at its east end, and a wide south aisle of the 1370s in length equal to five bays of the nave, plus a sixth bay corresponding to the central tower. The arcade has octagonal piers and arches with hoodmoulds and headstops. The were no transepts so the tower never had north and south openings of greater width than wide doorways which are set in blank arches. The east and west arches have boldly separated orders with wave-mouldings and filleted shafts with foliage capitals. The west window of the aisle could be original work of c1320 reset. Most of the other windows and the broach spire on the tower are of the 1850s but the roofs are late medieval and bear arms, badges and inscriptions referring to several families such as the Stanleys. The headless effigy of a late 14th century lady is presumably one of the Greys. There is also part of an effigy of an early 14th century priest. Later monuments include those of Gabriel Goodman, Dean of Westminster, d1601, John Parry, d1636, Gabriel Goodman, d1673, and several 18th century monuments of some note. There are also brasses to Dean Goodman's father Edward, 1560, and mother Ciselye, d1583. See plan on page 100.

The NE corner of Ruthin Church

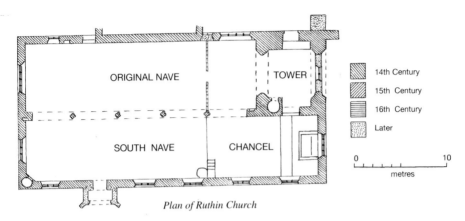

▨	14th Century
▨	15th Century
▤	16th Century
▨	Later

0   10
metres

Plan of Ruthin Church

ST ASAPH   *St Kentigern & St Asaph*   SJ 036743

The sandstone south nave with one original lancet is 13th century. The limestone north nave and the other windows and the hammer-beam roofs are of c1500. The south doorway is dated 1687, and the south porch, north vestry, and the bellcote on the south nave west wall are all of 1872. The five bay arcade has slender piers with keeled shafts and concave corners. There was once an inscription of 1524 on the west doorway. There is a tablet with four winged cherubs to Thomas Humphreys, d1698.

TRELAWNYD   *St Michael*   SJ 088796

The single chamber was remodelled in 1724 and 1895 leaving only parts of the side walls and the arch-braced roof with cusped struts above the collars. Of the 14th century are part of an heraldic grave slab in the vestry and the churchyard cross with a crucifixion scene in a cusped panel in the head. There is also an old octagonal font.

St Asaph Church

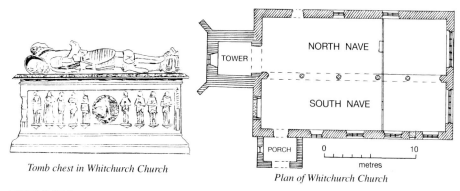

Tomb chest in Whitchurch Church

Plan of Whitchurch Church

TREMEIRCHION   *Corpus Christi (formerly Holy Trinity)*   SJ 083731

The west and north doorways of the single chamber are 14th century, as is the very fine tomb recess and effigy of the priest Dafydd ap Hywell ap Madog in the north wall. There are also a late 13th century effigy of a knight, possibly Sir Robert Pounderling, and fragments of grave-slabs of the same era. One south window is 15th century and one on the north is 17th century. Also on the north side are four heavy buttresses and a transept added in 1864. The other windows are of 1859 but the arch-braced roof is old. In the south windows are 15th and 17th century fragments of glass, including portraits of James I, Charles I, and John Williams, Archbishop of York.

TREUDDYN   *St Mary*   SJ 248582

The church was entirely rebuilt in 1874 but it contains a dug-out chest and there are minor remains of 14th and 16th century stained glass.

WHITCHURCH (LLANFARCHELL)   *St Marcella*   SJ 072662

This was originally the mother church of Denbigh. The south nave has a roll-moulded west doorway. A diagonally buttressed 16th century west tower has been added to the 15th century north nave. A window hoodmould stop shows a bearded man with long hair, ie probably early 16th century. One window is of c1600. The panelled roofs have arch-braced trusses and hammer beams alternating. The screens and altar rails are partly made from medieval material. The font is of 1640, the altar tables are of 1617 and 1623, the pulpit and tester are dated 1683, the chest is of 1676, and the benefaction board is of 1720. A brass depicts Richard Middleton, d1575, governor of Denbigh castle and his wife and family. There are effigies of Sir John Salusbury of Lleweni, d1578 and his wife and several other monuments, plus a series of nine hatchments.

WHITFORD   *St Mary & St Beuno*   SJ 146782

The north aisle with its roof, and six bay arcade and one window is 16th century. The middle two piers were replaced in the 1840s when the nave, south aisle and west tower were built. The font is dated 1649. There are chandeliers of 1755 and 1756, a Jacobean altar table, parts of 13th century grave-slabs, a dug-out chest, two pillar stones (one of which is to Bona, wife of Nobilis in the 6th century) and a medieval stone coffin. The monuments include tablets to Ellis Wynn, d1619, and Richard Coytmore, d1683, an incised slab to Elizabeth Mostyn, d1647, and a tablet to the historian Thomas Pennant, d1798.

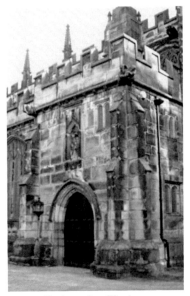

Worthenbury Church   *North porch at Wrexham*

WORTHENBURY   *St Deiniol*   SJ 419462

As rebuilt by Richard Trubshaw in 1736-9 the Early Georgian church at Worthenbury is the finest and best preserved of its type in Wales. It has a west tower, a coved ceiling and an east apse with Ionic and Corinthian pilasters inside. There are clasping pilasters on the outer corners and the round-arched windows have projecting frames with key-stones. The east window has fragments of stained glass from a Jesse window of 1393 formerly at Winchester college. The box-pews, pulpit and tester, etc, are all contemporary with the church, and there is a monument to Broughton Whitehall, d1734.

WREXHAM   *St Giles*   SJ 335501

This is one of the largest and finest medieval parish churches in Wales. The six-bay arcades plus some of the lower outer walling of the aisles and a piscina on the south side are of the period after an early tower fell down c1330. There was a fire in 1457 or 1463 and remodelling began under patronage of the Stanley family in the 1480s, the aisle windows and upper walls and the clerestory being of that period. A polygonal apse was added c1500 and the huge west tower bears an inscription of 1506, although work upon the upper parts continued until at least the 1520s. It has blank panelling, thirty statues in niches, crocketted ogival-headed openings, and pinnacles with openwork turrets on the corners. The tower connects with the nave by a single bay ante-nave flanked on the north side by an original early 16th century porch and on the south side by narrower second porch added in 1822.

The brass eagle lectern was given in 1524. Over the chancel arch are traces of a Last Judgement wall-painting of c1520. The oldest of the many monuments are those to Hugh Bellot, Bishop of Chester, d1596, the Reverend Thomas Myddelton, d1754, and his wife Arabella, Mary Myddelton, c1751, Sir Richard Lloyd, d1676, Ann Wilkinson, d1756 and the early 14th century knight Cynwrig ap Hywell.

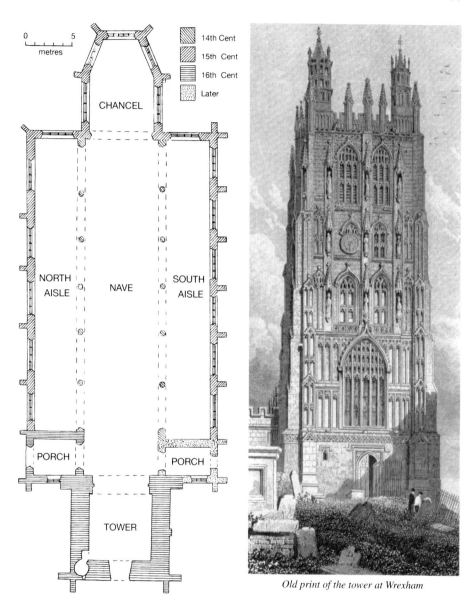

0   5
metres

▨ 14th Cent
▧ 15th Cent
▤ 16th Cent
▦ Later

CHANCEL

NORTH AISLE   NAVE   SOUTH AISLE

PORCH   PORCH

TOWER

Plan of Wrexham Church

Old print of the tower at Wrexham

YSGEIFIOG   *St Mary*   SJ 152715

In the west porch of the church of 1836 is an upright 14th century effigy of a priest. The octagonal base and part of the shaft remain of the former churchyard cross.

FURTHER READING

Abbeys, Priories & Cathedrals of Wales, Mike Salter 2012
Clwyd (Buildings of Wales series), Edward Hubbard, 1986
Gwynedd (Buildings of Wales series) R. Haslam, J. Orbach and A. Voelcker, 2009
Royal Commission on Ancient and Historical Monuments inventories for:
   Anglesey, Caernarvonshire, Denbighshire, Flintshire & Merioneth

INDEX OF CHURCHES

GLOSSARY OF TERMS

Apse	-	A semi-circular chapel or a similarly shaped east end of a church.
Ashlar	-	Masonry of large blocks cut to even faces and square edges.
Bays	-	Divisions of an elevation defined by regular vertical features.
Cartouche	-	A tablet with an ornate frame, usually enclosing an inscription.
Celure	-	Enriched area of the roof above a high altar or rood screen.
Chancel	-	The eastern member of a church reserved for priests and choristers.
Chevrons	-	Vs usually arranged in a continuous sequence to form a zigzag.
Claustral	-	To do with or belonging to a cloister.
Clerestory	-	An upper storey pierced by windows lighting the floor below.
Collar-Beam	-	A tie-beam used higher up near to the apex of a roof.
Corbel	-	A projecting or overhanging stone bracket.
Crossing Tower	-	A tower built upon four arches in the middle of a cruciform church.
Cruciform Church	-	Cross-shaped church with transepts forming the arms of the cross.
Cusps	-	Projecting points between the foils of a foiled Gothic arch.
Dado	-	Lower part of a wall, or its decorative treatment.
Dog-tooth	-	Four cornered stars placed diagonally and raised pyramidally.
Doric	-	One of the orders of Classical architecture of Greece and Rome.
Elizabethan	-	Of the time of Queen Elizabeth I (1558-1603)
Fleuron	-	Decorative carved shape like a flower or leaf.
Foil	-	A lobe formed by the cusping of a circle or arch.
Four-Centred Arch	-	A low, flat arch with each curve drawn from two compass points.
Hammerbeam Roof	-	Roof carried on arched braces set on beams projecting from a wall.
Head Stops	-	Heads of humans or beasts forming the ends of a hoodmould.
Hoodmould	-	A narrow band of stone projecting out over a window or doorway.
Impost	-	A wall bracket, often moulded, to support the end of an arch.
Jacobean	-	Of the time of King James I (1603-25).
Jamb	-	The side of a window, doorway or other opening.
Lancet	-	A long and comparatively narrow window, usually pointed headed.
Misericord	-	Hinged choir stall seat with a small lip to support a standing person.
Mullion	-	A vertical member dividing the lights of a window.
Nave	-	The part of a church in which the lay congregation stood or sat.
Ogival Arch	-	Topped by a curve which is partly convex and partly concave.
Pilaster	-	Flat buttress or pier attached to a wall. Used mainly in 12th century.
Piscina	-	The projecting base of a wall.
Plinth	-	A stone basin used for rinsing out holy vessels after a mass.
Quoin	-	A cut stone used to form part of a corner.
Respond	-	Half pier bonded into a wall and carrying one end of an arch.
Reticulation	-	Window tracery with a net-like appearance.
Rococo	-	The latest phase of the Baroque style, current c1720-60 in Britain.
Rood Screen	-	A screen with a crucifix mounted on it between a nave and a chancel.
Sedilia	-	Seats for clergy (usually three in the south wall of a chancel or choir.
Spandrel	-	The surface between two arches or between an arch and a corner.
Tester	-	A sounding board above a 17th or 18th century pulpit.
Tracery	-	The intersecting ribwork in the upper part of a Gothic window.
Transept	-	A cross-arm projecting at right-angles from a main body of a church.
Transom	-	A horizontal member dividing upper and lower lights in a window.
Voussoir	-	Small wedge-shaped stone used to help form an arch.
Wall-Plate	-	A timber laid longitudinally along the top of a wall.
Wind-Braces	-	The struts used to strengthen the sloping sides of a roof.

MAP OF CHURCHES IN GWYNEDD

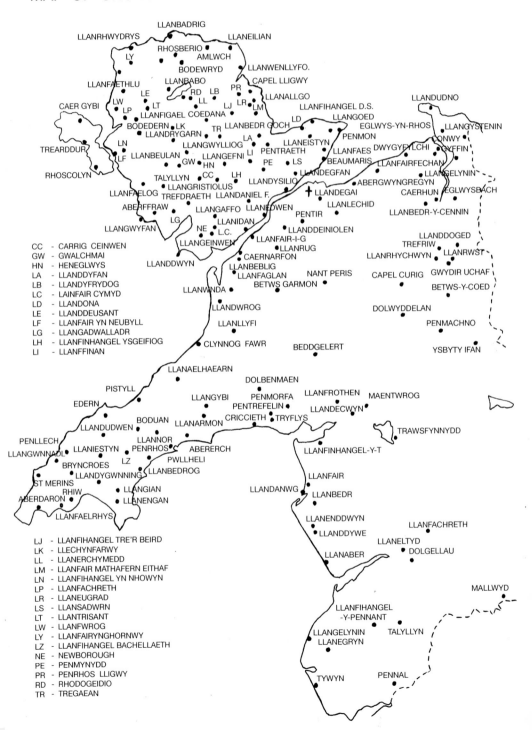

LLANBADRIG
LLANRHWYDRYS
LLANEILIAN
RHOSBERIO
LY   AMLWCH
BODEWRYD
LLANFAETHLU   LLANBABO   LLANWENLLYFO.
LE   RD   LB   PR   CAPEL LLIGWY
CAER GYBI   LW   LT   LL   LJ   LR   LM   LLANALLGO
LP   LLANFIGAEL COEDANA   LLANFIHANGEL D.S.   LLANDUDNO
BODEDERN   LK   LD   LLANGOED   EGLWYS-YN-RHOS   LLANGYSTENIN
LN   LLANDRYGARN   TR   LLANBEDR GOCH   DWYGYFYLCHI   CONWY
TREARDDUR   LF   LA   PENMON   GYFFIN
LLANBEULAN   LLANGWYLLIOG   LLANEISTYN   LLANFAES   LLANFAIRFECHAN
RHOSCOLYN   GW   LLANGEFNI   LI   PENTRAETH   BEAUMARIS   LLANGELYNIN
HN   PE   LS   LLANDEGFAN   ABERGWYNGREGYN
TALYLLYN   CC   LH   LLANDYSILIO   CAERHUN   EGLWYSBACH
LLANFAELOG   LLANGRISTIOLUS   LLANDEGAI
ABERFFRAW   TREFDRAETH   LLANDANIEL F.   LLANLECHID   LLANBEDR-Y-CENNIN
LG   LLANGAFFO   LLANEDWEN   PENTIR
LLANGWYFAN   NE   LLANIDAN   LLANDDEINIOLEN   LLANDDOGED
L.C.   TREFRIW   LLANRWST
LLANGEINWEN   LLANFAIR-I-G   LLANRUG   LLANRHYCHWYN
LLANDDWYN   CAERNARFON   GWYDIR UCHAF
LLANBEBLIG   NANT PERIS   CAPEL CURIG   BETWS-Y-COED
LLANFAGLAN   BETWS GARMON
LLANWNDA   DOLWYDDELAN
LLANDWROG   PENMACHNO
LLANLLYFI
CLYNNOG FAWR   BEDDGELERT   YSBYTY IFAN
LLANAELHAEARN
PISTYLL   DOLBENMAEN
EDERN   LLANGYBI   PENMORFA   LLANFROTHEN   MAENTWROG
PENTREFELIN   LLANDECWYN
BODUAN   CRICCIETH   TRYFLYS
LLANDUDWEN   LLANARMON   TRAWSFYNNYDD
PENLLECH   LLANNOR   LLANFINHANGEL-Y-T
LLANGWNNADL   LLANIESTYN   PENRHOS   ABERERCH
LZ   PWLLHELI   LLANFAIR
BRYNCROES   LLANBEDROG   LLANDANWG   LLANBEDR
LLANDYGWNNING
ST MERINS   RHIW   LLANGIAN   LLANENDDWYN   LLANFACHRETH
ABERDARON   LLANENGAN   LLANDDYWE   LLANELTYD
LLANFAELRHYS   LLANABER   DOLGELLAU
LLANFIHANGEL   MALLWYD
-Y-PENNANT
LLANGELYNIN   TALYLLYN
LLANEGRYN
TYWYN   PENNAL

CC - CARRIG CEINWEN
GW - GWALCHMAI
HN - HENEGLWYS
LA - LLANDDYFAN
LB - LLANDYFRYDOG
LC - LAINFAIR CYMYD
LD - LLANDONA
LE - LLANDDEUSANT
LF - LLANFAIR YN NEUBYLL
LG - LLANGADWALLADR
LH - LLANFINHANGEL YSGEIFIOG
LI - LLANFFINAN

LJ - LLANFIHANGEL TRE'R BEIRD
LK - LLECHYNFARWY
LL - LLANERCHYMEDD
LM - LLANFAIR MATHAFERN EITHAF
LN - LLANFIHANGEL YN NHOWYN
LP - LLANFACHRETH
LR - LLANEUGRAD
LS - LLANSADWRN
LT - LLANTRISANT
LW - LLANFWROG
LY - LLANFAIRYNGHORNWY
LZ - LLANFIHANGEL BACHELLAETH
NE - NEWBOROUGH
PE - PENMYNYDD
PR - PENRHOS LLIGWY
RD - RHODOGEIDIO
TR - TREGAEAN